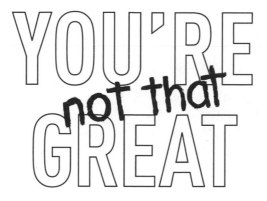

YOU'RE not that GREAT

(but neither is anyone else)

elan gale

GRAND CENTRAL
PUBLISHING

NEW YORK   BOSTON

Grand Central Publishing
Hachette Book Group
1290 Avenue of the Americas, New York, NY 10104
grandcentralpublishing.com
twitter.com/grandcentralpub

First Edition: December 2017

Grand Central Publishing is a division of Hachette Book Group, Inc. The Grand Central Publishing name and logo is a trademark of Hachette Book Group, Inc.

The publisher is not responsible for websites (or their content) that are not owned by the publisher.

The Hachette Speakers Bureau provides a wide range of authors for speaking events. To find out more, go to www.hachettespeakersbureau.com or call (866) 376-6591.

Handlettering by Brian Lemus.

Library of Congress Cataloging-in-Publication Data has been applied for.

ISBNs: 978-1-4789-1829-5 (hardcover), 978-1-4789-1832-5 (ebook)

Printed in the United States of America

LSC-C

10 9 8 7 6 5 4 3 2 1

For my mother, who once told me:
"As long as you're alive and breathing, and
as long as good things are happening,
shitty things will happen too"

contents

chapter one

you're not that great

We're not born laughing. We're born screaming.

—Brannon Braga (producer, director, screenwriter)

Let me tell you the story of you.

A long, long time ago, a man and a woman looked at each other and said, "Well, that's good enough." They fell in love, or at least they liked each other enough to want to get naked in the same room. Either the first night they met, or maybe a few months later, the man put his penis into the woman's vagina and gave her three relatively unpleasant minutes of grunting and sweating and thrusting before rolling onto his back and feeling pretty good about himself, while the woman regretted ever giving him her phone number. As the woman lay there, wondering why this man couldn't even bring her halfway to orgasm, a tiny little sperm somehow lazily stumbled towards an egg and weaseled its way in.

Those two people are your mother and father. That is how you were created. You are likely the result of two people being "whatever" about each other and deciding not to put latex between their genitals.

The following nine months you lived inside your mother, stealing most of her nutrients and generally making her feel sick and woozy. She had to quit drinking and smoking and missed out on a lot of the things she wanted to do because you were growing inside of her, kicking intermittently for no fucking reason. You just swam around in there, contributing nothing, and sucking vitamins through a tube like some kind of vampire. Literally, you began your life as a leech.

Finally, one glorious day, once you'd drained your mother of her last ounce of joy and energy, you decided to go ahead and make your grand entrance into the world. What followed was ten or so gruesome hours of screaming and general genital discomfort. No matter how great you think you are, it's important that you remember that your first act in this beautiful world was to cause the highest possible amount of pain to the person who loved you the most. Nice work.

The immediate future wasn't much better, to be honest. You spent the next three years as a waste-manufacturing facility. When you weren't making unpleasant sounds, you were making unpleasant smells, shitting and pissing and vomiting everywhere. You made abundantly sure that your parents never slept. You made them feed you every few hours, which for your mother often demanded public nudity. Any gift you were given, you would put in your mouth and then immediately throw onto the floor. Basically, you made sure to make every single moment of your parents' lives difficult while offering little reward other than the promise that maybe, one day, you'd turn into a worthwhile person. This is how you treated the people who spent every waking hour just trying to keep you alive.

To strangers, you were no better. You ruined dinner for count-less families in countless restaurants and your mere presence made the already dreary business of air travel even more unbearable. Your incessant wailing, your tantrums, your screaming bloody murder, went on for years.

But not to worry, you would soon escape infancy and become a child and surely you would finally become something worth-while, right? You would become self-sufficient and selfless in no time, right?

Well, not quite. Instead you just became a bottomless money pit. School supplies, new clothes, and birthday parties drained your parents' bank accounts. Playdates, sleepovers, and thank-less PTA meetings wasted countless hours of their lives. On top of that, you began to develop emotionally and required constant coddling. You demanded to be told that you were a "good boy" or a "good girl" when in fact you were pretty terrible. But instead of sitting you down on your little ass and telling you that you were slowly killing them, your parents encouraged this selfishness.

The very first bit of respite your parents got from the twenty-four-hour nightmare that was raising you came when you were old enough to begin your education. You were finally sent to school (which gave your parents a chance to just feel alive again and maybe fuck without you in earshot) and while there you would make drawings. And these "drawings"—if you can even call them that—weren't just bad; they were total garbage. You were asked to draw a house and your parents, and what you ended up with looked like two malformed hot dogs in front of a big brown cube. And you probably drew a ridiculous sun in the corner like some kind of idiot who has no sense of scale and no idea that if the sun were really that close it would burn all of our skin off.

This is where things went from bad to worse.

When you came home from school with that disgusting drawing in your hand, your parents should have lit the page on fire and duct-taped your fingers together to make sure that you never got it in your mind to pick up a crayon again. But something told them not to do that. Something deep down inside told your parents not to be truthful with you. So instead of looking you square in the eyes and telling you to keep trying until it wasn't such a piece of shit, they smiled at you and taped your monstrous masterpiece to the refrigerator door. They told you that they were proud of you and called you their "little artist." And you felt so good about yourself.

And on that day, they turned you into the self-loving, egomaniacal monster that you are today!

The day your horrendous ego was born, it began whispering sweet nothings to you from inside your head. It's the little voice inside that tells you that you deserve to have a good life. It's the voice inside that tells you that you are special. It's the voice that tells you that you are strong and powerful and can have anything you want. It tells you that you're good enough, you're smart enough, and doggone it, people like you.

From the day you brought your garbage artwork home from school to yesterday when your friends lied to you and told you that you look good in those pants, that voice has been growing and growing, larger and larger, and now it is the only voice you hear and the only voice you trust. You somehow believe that you are destined for big things. You believe that you're special. You believe that you're important.

And that's how we got to where we are today.

That is your story. That is the story of you. At least until now. Because now your story is about to change.

You were a helpless screeching pile of flesh with feces coming out of your bottom at an alarming rate, and other than the fact that you're a little bit taller, maybe have a college degree, and "love yourself," not much has changed. So it's time to quiet the lying voice that lives in your brain and face the reality:

You're Not That Great.

who are you?

If you're reading this book, chances are pretty good that you're doing okay. I mean, let's be honest, books aren't cheap, so you probably have a job. In order to get to that job, you probably have a car. It's probably not the car you always wanted, but it probably has seats and doors, so that's pretty good. Oh, and if you're reading this book, it means you know how to read. So that means you were lucky enough in life to get an education. That probably had very little to do with you, honestly. That's just luck. In fact, most of the above is luck. You were born in a time when "having a job" didn't mean getting whipped half to death by an Egyptian man while you built a cute resting place for his uncle's body. You have time to complain about the temperature of your latte instead of dying of starvation like half of your ancestors. You have the energy to complain about how shitty the Wi-Fi is on airplanes, while the people who lived here before you died of dysentery just trying to deliver a love letter to someone two states over. You are living your best life. The world is your oyster and you absolutely expect every oyster you open to be home to a pearl.

THAT'S TRUE, AND THAT ALL SOUNDS PRETTY GREAT! SO WHAT IS WRONG WITH ME, THEN?

Look, I don't know you personally, but there's probably a

whole hell of a lot wrong with you. I mean, so many things that we don't have time to list all your issues. You probably have daddy issues. You probably fear abandonment. You are probably jealous and envious and you're probably too prideful to admit any of this. You're probably not as successful or as productive as you want to be. You're probably reading this book right now thinking, "Why the fuck am I reading this book if it's just going to keep insulting me?" but you also know that deep down you have all of these issues. Because WE ALL have these issues.

So if we all have these issues, they're not so bad, right? Well, I guess it depends on what you want. If you're happy with having what everyone else has, then, yes, it's fine. Just go ahead and admit that your spirit animal is the ostrich and stick your head in the sand and pretend you're doing okay. But if you already had everything you wanted, you wouldn't be here with me right now. No, you'd be pleasuring yourself in a warm bath and eating chocolate cake without an ounce of guilt. So let's get started, shall we?

who am i?

I'm just like you. I am insecure. I have abandonment issues. I have daddy issues. I have body dysmorphia and anxiety and I'm a germaphobe and sometimes I use run-on sentences. I am a giant mass of nerves and tissue and problems. Just like you. But unlike some people, I know that my problems are the best and most important parts of me. They're what make me *me*. I am my problems. And you are yours...

I'm not telling you anything you don't know. You KNOW you have all these issues, and most likely at this point in your life you've had a few nights where a couple of cheap glasses of Chardonnay led to you calling up a friend at three o'clock in the morning, crying and screaming, "I don't know what's wrong with me." You've slept with someone you didn't really like just to feel alive. And you've definitely ordered enough Chinese food for six people and pretended it wasn't just for you, and yelled, "I'll be right there," into an empty living room just to hide your deep, deep shame.

But here's what you don't know. And this is the thing that will kill you (even faster than the sodium content of that pork lo mein):

You're an addict.

And your drug of choice is POSITIVITY. You listen to the voice in your head because you like what it has to say. You want to be HAPPY. You want to believe that you are SPECIAL and IMPORTANT. You NEED it. You CRAVE it. You are hopelessly and totally committed to FEELING GOOD when really you should be focused on BEING BETTER.

But alas, there's your old friend: positivity. You've been told that positivity is the thing that's going to fix all your problems. You've been told (since the day your parents hung your trash-drawing on the refrigerator) that positivity is the thing that you can't live without. You've been told that positivity is the new penicillin.

But positivity isn't the cure. It's the disease.

chapter two

the power of positive thinking

My therapist once told me, "You're not a beauty; you're average. You're not talented; you're lucky." She said I needed to accept my limitations to overcome my perfectionism. But it had the opposite effect; I WOULD PROVE HER WRONG!! This method worked until the day she told me that she'd never had a patient kill themselves and my first thought was "challenge accepted!" I no longer see her.

—Nikki Glaser (comedian)

What feels better than a compliment? Nothing.

A compliment is like a hug for your brain. Actually, it's more than a hug. It's like a full-on night of hot and heavy lovemaking. No, really. In an article for *Tonic*, K. Aleisha Fetters notes that when you get a compliment, the same part of your brain lights up that lights up when you're having sex. It's even been theorized that compliments trigger dopamine to be released, causing you to feel immense pleasure. Dopamine is also linked to addiction, though. Compliments work like nicotine, at first giving you a thrill, but eventually making you totally dependent on them. Where are the after-school specials to help get kids off compliments?

Positivity is a drug, but unlike hugs (which are awesome), positivity is dangerous because it's just SO damn addictive.

It's been a part of you for so long that you can't even remember a time you weren't totally dependent on it. Before you even knew how to wipe your own ass, your parents would sit you there on your little miniature toilet and clap and sing and dance for you. They'd congratulate you for taking a shit, as if that isn't something that literally every living thing does. You may have gotten older, but your need to get a round of applause every time you take that proverbial shit hasn't dissipated.

Even now you're probably feeling a little uncomfortable because you're used to reading self-help books that tell you how wonderful and charming and great you already are and are so complimentary that they may as well just be licking your genitals as they take your money like a prostitute (an apt comparison, frankly).

But all those self-help books and all your positive friends and all your daily affirmations aren't going to curb your desperate need for approval. In fact, it just gets worse and worse every day, as those around you fill your brain with so much self-loving bliss it's surprising you can get your bloated head through a doorway. Let's face it, you likely can't even eat an omelet without posting it on Instagram and getting "likes." And don't even try to blame social media for making you so dependent on praise. Those systems were built because the engineers knew exactly what you needed to feel happy and fulfilled. This inevitably leads to you connecting your phone to an exercise app that lets everyone you're friends with on Facebook know how many miles you've run this week. You write reviews of all your favorite places so strangers can benefit from your "exceptionally good" taste. You put on a pair of pants and ask ten people how they look. And I'm willing to bet if someone tells you that you look like crap (which you probably do) they get told that their words are hurtful, and then they'll never be honest with you again.

You need it. You crave it. You desire it. But you're not willing to work for it. You want to be praised for who you already are and you don't care if people actually mean it or not. And you praise people for who they already are, even if deep down in your soul you know there's a whole lot of room for improvement. Why do you do that?

You do it because you don't want to be negative, and you've been told that negativity is bad. You do it because you don't want to hurt their feelings. And you do it because you know that it's always a lot easier to be nice and sweet and kind than it is to be honest.

But have you ever considered that for every time you look at someone and don't tell him or her that their horrible haircut is an abomination that even God couldn't forgive, ten people are probably doing that right back to you? So what has the world become? With all the likes and the retweets and the compliments that nobody means. It's a world of contentment. A world of mediocrity. A world of average people who think they're excellent.

If you're okay with being mediocre, I have good news for you: You're already there. But if you want to excel and actually do interesting things, you're going to have to get motivated.

And let me tell you what DOESN'T motivate you: POSITIVITY.

Positivity is a very pleasant thing to be around if you're happy exactly where you are, but if you're looking to get things done, positivity is like a giant hammock you just can't seem to get out of. If you want to make an actual change to your life, you need to use one of the more motivating emotions, like anger, rage, desperation, or revenge. Positivity doesn't cause those feelings, but *negativity* sure does.

No matter who you are, your life is full of "negative" emotions. You can't get away from them. I mean, you can try by being positive and full of shit all the time, but life is full of some ups and A LOT of downs. And this book wants to help you use those downs. This book is here to help you turn those "negative" emotions into action that will make you better instead of just feeling better about who you already are. It won't make you *feel* good, but it might make you *be* good.

To do that, negativity is exactly what you need. Think back to your youth. What got you more motivated when you were a kid? The really nice boy who invited everyone to his birthday party or the asshole bully who lit your books on fire and you'd run home crying but then you'd also be daydreaming about how one day you were going to be bigger and you were going to buy a bulldozer and you were going to drive straight to his family's house and tear down the front wall while he was in the bathroom so everyone in the neighborhood would see him on the toilet?

The feeling you got when someone picked on you or told you that you weren't good enough or told you that you would never be anything: those are the things that gave you the strength you needed to rise up and fight against something. There is a lot of power in having other people dislike you. There is a lot of power in having other people not believe in you. There is a lot of power in people telling you that you're never going to be the things you want to be.

But you've done *such* a good job of cleansing all of these forces from your life. You've smoothed over every conflict and "been the bigger person" to end every fight. You've loudly declared, "I don't have time for negative people in my life," when in reality those are the people you really needed all along. And maybe it's not that you didn't like all those people. Maybe you were just aware of what their words meant. Maybe you knew that the things they said were hurting your feelings because those things resonated so deeply with you. Maybe you didn't want anyone to tell you that you weren't good enough because you knew they were right. Was it "negativity" really? Or was it truth? And if it was just negativity, why didn't you just brush it off? If it didn't really hit you in a soft spot, why did you run from it?

It's entirely possible that the "negative people" in your life were just assholes. Sure, there are bad people with bad intentions out there. But most people aren't smart enough to have an agenda. They're just saying what they're thinking and observing. When most people are being critical, they're just telling you how the world sees you. If you don't like what they have to say, that's fine. But instead of ignoring them, think about the things they're being critical of! Turn your hurt feelings off for half a second and ask yourself this: "Are they right?" If they are, now is your chance to change. Now is your chance to make them wrong. Don't ignore the haters; use the haters to make yourself better, constantly evolving, constantly changing, until you're so much fucking better than they ever imagined you could be. And after all of that, if they're still negative, then you tell them to fuck the fuck off.

Thankfully, even if you've been successful at purging all the negative people from your life, you still have access to the most destructive and violent force of all: yourself.

No one can possibly dislike you as much as you can dislike yourself. That's because no one knows you as well as you know yourself, and the more you get to know about yourself, the more likely you are to be able to be hypercritical. You can hide your flaws from all your "friends," but you can't ever fully kill off the other, more honest little voice inside of you that says exactly how you feel about yourself. When you finally unleash the surging pile of built-up self-loathing that lives inside your head, you'll find yourself significantly more capable of actually doing the things you want to do.

But first you need to rid yourself of positivity. And before you dismiss positive thinking entirely, it's important that you get a real sense of exactly what positive thinking can do! POSITIVE THINKING is, in fact, one of the most powerful forces in the world. Let me tell you the story of my friend James from Vermont.

James didn't have much of a family. His mother left when he was a child and of course his father was overwhelmed, between working two jobs and raising a young lad all on his own. He didn't have time to teach James about the power of positive thinking. Positive thinking was a luxury that was only afforded to people who ALREADY had it all. He could only teach James about things like "hard work" and "dedication," but as we all know, those things aren't enough. To succeed you don't really have to work hard. You just need to think that you're great and feel like you're worthwhile. You need to know that you deserve it. You need to say it aloud in the mirror every morning whenever you feel like waking up and you need to say it to anyone who can stand to be around you. I AM GOOD. I AM GOOD. I AM GREAT. I AM SOARING. I AM A PHOENIX AND EVEN IN DEATH I WILL RISE AGAIN.

Things were going alright for James. He had a job at a great local pizza place, serving up handmade calzones, and he was working on his college degree. He wasn't exactly sure what he wanted to do with his life yet, but he knew that if he worked hard and persisted, just like his father had taught him, he would find a way in this complicated world. But in 2006 he heard about something new: The Power of Positive Thinking. And this very discovery would change the course of his life forever.

Apparently, you didn't really need to work hard for the things you wanted. Apparently, the reason why you didn't have these things was because the Universe didn't know that you wanted them. It was your *fault for not putting out the correct energy. This new theory postulated that the Universe would always give you back the energy you put out. (We know this now to be true, of course, because everyone who puts their desire into the Universe gets exactly what they want. Literally, every single asshole who paid $24.99 for a book about this lives in a giant mega-mansion and is president of the moon.) For James, this changed everything.*

Secretly, James had always had one desire. He had always wanted to be a DJ. He wanted to stand in front of crowds of thousands and really make them dance and party and do hard-core drugs and have a good time. And at the end of the night all those thousands of people would be thankful to him for the totally bodacious time they'd just had. And also he would get to have sex with a bunch of young groupies. He'd never gone after this dream because, well, he had bills to pay. DJ equipment costs money, and on top of all that, he really didn't have any musical talent. But this new theory taught him that he didn't have to really learn how to be a DJ; he just needed to want to be a DJ hard enough and eventually the world would reward his desires (as it always does, but ONLY if you buy the hardcover, not if you buy some cheap paperback edition) for fame and fortune.

Finally, James took the plunge. He dropped out of college, quit his job at the pizza joint, and proclaimed loudly to all of his friends: "I'm going to be a DJ." No one thought he knew how to be a DJ, but he was so insistent, so confident, so determined that there was no way this was not *going to happen for him, that they tried to be supportive. His friends sat him down and tried to tell him things like, "You don't know how to be a DJ" and "Do you have any records? Or a record player?" but he would not be distracted by the **haters**. He kept showing up at clubs. He kept making fliers with his new DJ name and a picture of him on them.*

He did all the things a person who was a DJ would probably do, other than actually DJ. But above all else, he told himself that he was great. Even when he was out of money and had to move into his ex– college roommate's uncle's basement in Glendale, even then he declared, "I am going to be the most famous DJ of all time," and even when he couldn't get his job back at the pizza parlor and had to get a job selling discount condoms, cigarettes, and gum at a Shell station, he told every customer, "I am going to be the most famous DJ of all time," and even when he got banned from pretty much every club in the city for trying to bring his equipment onstage even though he didn't have a gig there, he still declared, "I am going to be the most famous DJ of all time. I AM GREAT I AM GOOD I AM THE BEST I WILL SUCCEED IF IT'S THE LAST THING I DO. I HAVE THE POWER OF POSITIVE THINKING ON MY SIDE AND NOTHING WILL STOP ME!"

He refused to give up. He refused to surrender. He refused to quit! He never stopped putting his desire out into the Universe. He never stopped believing in himself. He NEVER stopped THINKING POSITIVELY. Ever. Never. Not for anyone.

And do you know who that man is today?

No. No, you don't.

That's because he's an assistant payroll accountant for a pharmaceutical company in a small suburb outside of Knoxville, Tennessee. He is in charge of helping with payroll issues for the much more successful people who go from office to office selling Viagra and Chantix to greedy doctors. He lives with his wife, whom he hates, and his children, who wish to "not grow up to be like Daddy because he's sad all the time." Now he sits at home on Sundays and prays to the Universe that turned a deaf ear to all of his endless pleas. No one in his life now knows who he really is. Or who he thought he was going to be. They don't believe in him. And they're right. Because he never did anything. He never learned to do anything other than think positively. He didn't need to. That was supposed to be enough.

And that, my friends, is the power of positive thinking.

Now, this is not to say that there is no honor in being a payroll accountant. Or that there is no honor in selling condoms or gum. Nothing could be further from the truth. The kind of success I'm talking about is personal. It has to be. Not everyone can be Beyoncé or Marissa Mayer or Elon Musk, but not everyone wants to be either. The sadness you should feel for James is not that he didn't do the work necessary to live up to *your* expectations. It's that he didn't do the work to live up to **his own**. He didn't do any of the things that *he* wanted to do. So before you get too worried and think that you're being asked to be a successful billionaire or a world-renowned rock star, this isn't about that. It's simply about pushing yourself towards the limits of *your own* desires and capabilities.

You only get one life. (Hopefully. This shit is exhausting and there is no way I'd want to do it again.) And what is a bigger slap in the face to *all of the Universe* than wasting it? So what do you want to do with it?

Do that.

I always knew I wanted to be in entertainment. I always knew I had a lot to say and I wanted a lot of people to listen to me. To be honest, most of that desire comes from deeply felt insecurities that existed before I even knew how to identify them. I gravely fear death and I don't want my life to be meaningless and I knew I wanted to leave something tangible behind. I guess I could've tried to be president, but I also have a modicum of morality, so that was pretty much out of the question.

I was never sure I wanted to have kids and I was also so remarkably afraid of dying that I never thought I'd live long enough to get married and have a family, so writing something or directing something or producing something that people would talk about and reference and remember was my only hope for a little taste of life after death. TV and movies could live on long after I was gone. I was pretty determined.

Since I was a little kid, there have been a lot of people who encouraged me. Friends and family would listen to me talk and tell me how great I was and how easy it was going to be for me to find an audience for whatever I wanted to do. But how could I trust any of those people? They seemed to tell everyone the same thing: that they were great.

Remember when *American Idol* was one of the biggest shows on television? Even though we hate to admit it, we were all only marginally interested in people singing well. Sure it's cool when someone can impressively belt out Aerosmith's "Sweet Emotion," but if you REALLY wanted to hear that song sung well, you could just listen to Steven Tyler. We watched it and loved it because there was something so cathartic and weirdly painful about the audition process. Once in a while, it was fun to hear someone defy all odds and kick ass, but really the most fun was in listening to someone who was entirely full of themselves completely tank.

It was always the same. Some guy or girl in their early twenties would walk into the room with Simon, Randy, and Paula with some incredible swagger. You could feel the confidence before they even spoke a word, and they would proudly declare that they were going to sing some difficult ballad and knock the judges' fucking socks off. Randy would raise an eyebrow and then it would begin: this cacophonous nightmare coming out of someone's mouth. Paula would be the first to spit up her sponsored Coke; Simon would attempt to stop the dying cat from screaming. And then the judges would lay into them, telling this fool how horrifying and ghastly their performance was. And every single time, the person auditioning couldn't hear it. They never said, "Oh my god, I can't believe I've been subjecting family and friends to this for so long. I am a living, breathing nightmare and I should be put down." No, they always said, "I'm great. You're wrong." And we would all turn to each other in our living rooms and we would ask, "What the fuck is wrong with this person?"

The answer to that question is pretty simple. They believed they were great because they were told that they were great. Friends, family members, and probably even strangers would rather tell someone they're great and move on with their lives than have to deal with the aftermath of telling someone they're not going to reach their dream. These relatives and friends certainly weren't being malicious. There's no question they thought they were doing the right thing by supporting this shitty, shitty singer.

But what they did to those people was wrong. It was cruel. They let them walk down the wrong path, over and over again, until the uncaring void swallowed them whole and they were never heard from again. Maybe that's a mild exaggeration. But at the very least, they were embarrassed as hell and wasted an unbelievable amount of time.

There are two ways to help people who have no chance of attaining their goals. One is to tell them to give up before they accidentally spend their whole lives climbing a mountain they have no chance of reaching the top of. And the other way is to tell them, "You're not that great. And if you ever want to be great, you have a whole shitload of work to do. You sound like a raccoon being run over by a car."

Now, this may seem harsh, but think about it this way: The only outcome after all those years of family and friends being supportive was that the singers FELT GOOD about themselves. And, sure, FEELING GOOD is fine and dandy, but the result of FEELING GOOD is that they NEVER GOT BETTER because they didn't know that THEY HAD TO. And those good feelings led them to follow their dreams until those dreams literally bit them in the asshole, on national television, in front of ten million people. I feel bad for those people. I do. And not because they've been embarrassed— because everyone gets embarrassed and then you get over it—but because they have to go home and look their loved ones in the eye, knowing that for years and years they'd been lied to.

So how could I possibly listen to the people who loved me when they told me I was great? And let's imagine that I did believe them. Other than FEELING GOOD, what does that really do for me? I remember that most of my friends, teachers, and relatives told me to keep going and I would find my place in the world. But to be honest, none of that was really very *helpful*. I already knew what I wanted to do and I knew I would keep trying because, while I actually enjoyed my job as a customer service representative at Hollywood Video and the occasional part-time catering gig, I knew I would do whatever it took to keep from doing those jobs forever.

But one person wasn't quite so confident in my ability to make all of my dreams come true. That was my father. He wasn't particularly negative and he was never mean about it, but he would encourage me to do literally ANYTHING other than try to make it in enter-tainment. More than anything, he wanted me to get a proper educa-tion so that when I failed, I would still have options. A backup plan.

All the many empty compliments and encouragements I got from the time I brought home my first shitty drawing have been long forgotten. But what I haven't forgotten is the time when my father let me know, in his attempt to truly help me, that making a living in entertainment was simply "not possible."

I was so mad. What gave him the right to talk to me that way? How could he dare to step outside the sacred circle of compli-ments and smoke blowing that we all constantly engage in? I needed to prove him wrong. But how?

I was about to go to college when he had this conversation with me. I was seventeen. And like a seventeen-year-old, I was angry and I was disbelieving. I was full of myself and egotistical and thought I had it really figured out. But I also didn't really have much recourse. I didn't have a better solution than to go off to college (although I guess my bullshit major of "film and visual culture" would show him!).

I didn't realize yet how unbelievably boring college would be for me. I had already been drinking heavily and smoking and having sex and all the fun things that I wasn't supposed to do, so college just felt like this sad place where people were pretending to be adults. I didn't join a fraternity, which meant there was no social life for me there, and I found myself with an endless amount of free time to sit around and think. And in those countless quiet hours in my shitty, tiny dorm room, I kept coming back to what my father had said: "Not possible."

And that's when I started making plans. I started writing every day. I started making short films and music videos and teaching myself how to edit. I taught myself to use Photoshop. I sold my services wherever possible. I wrote screenplays for a small independent start-up for free.

I started doing really poorly in all my classes, but luckily, I didn't give a shit. There was nothing I wanted at this college. The things I wanted were out of reach and I wasn't prepared to settle. I didn't learn to deal with the disappointment. I didn't learn to wait and see. I didn't learn to relax and let life take its course. I got angrier and angrier until I was ready to burst.

I had an enemy now: it wasn't my father; it was his opinion.

"Not possible." The idea that someone had told me what I couldn't accomplish made me the most energized, inspired lunatic anyone could imagine. I barely slept and I did ANYTHING and EVERYTHING I could to prove those words wrong.

Feeling good felt good, but nothing was as inspiring as feeling bad. The fear that overtook me when I was told I wasn't going to get to have the kind of life I wanted to have made me determined and powerful. It was SO important for me to prove those words wrong. I had an antagonist and a wall to climb and something to fight against. You'll never run faster than when a mugger is chasing you, and you'll never jump farther than when there are alligators snapping in the water beneath your feet.

There's no need to get into the specifics because everyone's path is going to be different, but what followed for the next few years could be distilled to one thing: a desire to be right. The backs of my eyelids were tattooed with the words "not possible," and instead of waking up every morning feeling refreshed and like I could accomplish anything, I woke up every morning angry that I hadn't achieved my goals yet. And so I slept less, because I didn't deserve sleep. And I skipped family trips because I didn't earn them. I stayed in the same shitty apartment for years because I didn't deserve a place without dog-shit stains on the carpet.

And then I started making a living in entertainment. And I got to be right and I got to feel like I earned something and feel like I deserved something. And I let myself sleep and I let myself take vacations. And I got to take those words, "not possible," and I got to shove them up the ass of anyone who would listen.

I was happy. For a minute. And then I realized that I had lost my enemy. I had lost the most energizing force in my life. My fear and my anger and my desire to be right were all that had lifted me up and carried me to this point. What could I possibly accomplish without those things?

And then something wonderful happened: I realized that it wasn't enough.

I had found a new addiction: negativity.

The addiction to positivity had a hold on me for so long, just like it has a hold on many of you. I was keeping one last little bit of positivity I could listen to. I would say to myself, "Good job. You did it. You proved everyone wrong." But that wasn't actually *useful*. It made me tired. It made me complacent. I realized I was hindering myself with my self-congratulatory vibes.

And so I started a new course of action in my life, focusing on all the things that were wrong with me and pounding myself with negative words and disaffirmations. That's why I can't even sit here and list my accomplishments now. I don't feel like any of my accomplishments are enough, and that's exactly the kind of negative feedback that gets me up every morning and makes me into the kind of person who others often see as "doing well."

Sure, I was making a living. I was doing the "not possible." But was I making the *best* living? Was I using *every* moment well? What *else* was wrong with me?

Well, I was alone. I was fat and out of shape. I was an out-of-check alcoholic slowly killing myself. I said these things (all of which were true, and all of which NO ONE ELSE WOULD TELL ME) over and over again until I replaced all of my feelings of complacency with feelings of anger, fear, despair, and sadness. After all, those were the things that got me to where I was now. Why give up? Why call it a life? Why not USE all those fucked-up feelings to build the best future possible?

I know what you're thinking, though. You're thinking, "What about being happy?" Well, being "happy" is overrated AND is a bullshit lie. More on that in Chapter Five, but first, let's talk about the feelings that matter. Let's talk about all the feelings that you need to live your best life.

Anger, sadness, fear, self-loathing, and desperation. Rage, fear of death, and revenge. These are the things that make for success.

And now you're going to stop hiding from them and start making them your bitch.

As I went through the process of writing this book, I had to be sure that all of my assertions about positivity, negativity, and success were right. I had to ask some questions of myself:

Am I just fucked up?

Maybe this particular brand of thinking really only works for someone like you?

Is this all bullshit?

So I started asking around. I talked to friends and acquaintances. I wrote to people I admired and I asked them to tell me what their experiences were with "negative" emotions and how those experiences played into their life stories.

I remembered reading about Scott Derrickson, who has been a successful film director for a long time, and about some of the hurdles he faced before he became internationally renowned for his ingenious Marvel film, *Doctor Strange*. Here is the conversation we had:

What emotion has most strongly fueled the drive to succeed in you?

In my case, fear has been the driving force in my life since childhood. I chose the horror genre as a means of exploring and understanding it better, and confronting my own fears. Both as a viewer and as a filmmaker, that genre has helped me face unspoken and unspeakable truths about myself and the world. To me, horror is the genre of non-denial.

When faced with "negative" emotions, how do you respond? Do you try to get over them or use them to drive your creativity?

I don't necessarily try to do either—I try to face them and understand them. Sometimes they are irrational or untruthful and need to be resisted, but sometimes they are the result of hard truths that need to be embraced and accepted.

Was there a low point for you in your career or personal life that made you better for having experienced it?

The failure of my film *The Day the Earth Stood Still* almost destroyed my career. For two years I wasn't getting much work as a writer and no work at all as a director. I was filled with extreme amounts of fear, which told me that my identity and security were too connected to my career. I made *Sinister* as a reaction to this fear in me—Ethan Hawke's character was the embodiment of who I did not want to be.

What's your favorite "negative" emotion and why?

Guilt. There is false guilt, but I don't experience that much. Guilt over my wrongdoings and shortcomings is an important negative emotion. If we don't embrace it and listen to it, how can we ever be driven to become better? I care more about growing into a better human being than being successful. I care more about meaning than happiness. I need my guilt to tell me that I need to correct my behavior. And by embracing it, I become more forgiving of other people.

What advice would you give to people who are insecure or fearful or desperate or sad?

Don't deny those feelings; go deeper into them. Confronting them is the only way to rise above them, and the suffering of the struggle over those feelings is the very thing that can shape you into the person you ought to be.

———

Scott is just one of many people I admire who doesn't cherry-pick his favorite emotions. He is a consumer of all life has to offer. Throughout this book, you will hear more stories of people I respect. Many of them agree with my philosophies, but more important, I learned more and more about myself by listening to each and every one of them. You should too, you idiot.

---

chapter three

all the stupid things you've been told

The first part of getting rid of any addiction is admitting that you have a problem. So take a deep breath and repeat after me:

> *I am addicted to positivity. I am addicted to positivity. I am*
> *addicted to positivity.*
> *I care more about **feeling** great than **being** great.*
> *I am NOT THAT GREAT.*

Okay, fantastic. You have now completed phase one of overcoming your dependence on feel-good bullshit, and you can get out of your stupid yoga pants, take the namaste sticker off your "meditation room" wall, and pour the home-brewed kombucha down the drain along with the last shred of your ill-deserved ego and begin anew!

What now, though? How do you move on, knowing that maybe the world doesn't give a shit about you being happy? Well, unfortunately, you're going to have to unlearn a lot of the things you've spent the last few years indoctrinating yourself with. It's likely that most of these things have entered your mind subliminally via Instagram, through terrible billboards, or from your dumb uncle Terry on Facebook. But through repetition (and because these things are easy and pleasant), these thoughts and feelings now live inside of you.

What are these mind traps I'm referring to?

Inspirational quotes.

Of course it's more than just that. You've been riddled with bad advice from the moment you were born until ten seconds before you picked up this book, and now you need to open your mind, look deep down inside, and take a long, hard (that's what she said?) look at the aphorisms you've heard so many times that you've started to believe them. They're part of our everyday life. They're part of our culture. And like many things that are part of our culture, they must be destroyed.

All of the most frequently used platitudes are confusing, vague, and, most important, at odds with one another. Now, look. I know you don't take ALL of these things literally, but words are important. So let's take a closer, literal look at some of these common phrases, and see how they would be practically applied:

Live Each Day as If It's Your Last—What would you do on your last day on Earth? The answer is: nothing productive. Some people would spend all of their money on the car they always wanted. Some people would finally get up the courage to sleep with that one coworker they always wanted to bang. Even more would ruin their marriage or tell the family member they hate how they really feel about them. The vast majority would spend their final few minutes on this planet crying hysterically in a ball on the floor and wishing the nightmare would end.

This is great advice, clearly. Cheat on your husband, buy a tank with your life savings, and crash it into the side of your boss's lake house. Yes, of course this statement is supposed to be hyperbole. No one is actually advising you to tie up your racist aunt and throw her off the side of the Grand Canyon. It's supposed to give you a "feeling," but the feeling is also wrong. It's oversimplified and it is basically a polite way of telling you that you are a simpleton and can't understand the complexities of life.

Dream as If You'll Live Forever—You know that dream you have? The one where you're three thousand years old and you've had the unique pleasure of living through every war and nuclear Armageddon humankind has unsuccessfully launched in its bid to destroy itself? The one where everyone you ever loved has died and then when you finally forget about them and manage to fall in love again the next person dies too, over and over again, with you endlessly losing everything you want until your only dream is for each day to be your last? Again, obviously, no one really means this. So why do they say it? Do they think you're too dumb to understand that it's important to have long-term plans but also take short-term actions to achieve them? Do they think you can't understand any advice that doesn't fit on a mug or on a funny T-shirt in a Des Moines home-goods shop?

Let Go and Let God—Try this one while driving on the highway and let me know how it goes.

Believe in Yourself—Really? Why? Someone who really should believe in themselves wouldn't be looking for motivation on Instagram. They would be building a bridge or running for Congress. Who is this for? Why have I never seen anyone I aspire to be like posting this online?

It Is What It Is!—I don't think there is a less meaningful sentence in the English language than this one. But people say it, and they mean it! Saying "it is what it is" is the intellectual equivalent of just opening your mouth, sticking your fist inside, and holding it there until you die of hunger. Of course it is what it is. That is exactly what it is. You're actually *not saying anything*. So don't say it. Imagine if other people used this phrase to try to help you:

You: Officer, someone broke into my house and took everything I own!

Officer: Unfortunately, we often never catch these people. I'm afraid all your things are gone forever. Do you have insurance?

You: No, I don't! This is terrible! Isn't this terrible?

Officer: Well, all I can tell you is that *it is what it is*.

You: What does that mean?

Officer: I have no idea. People just always say it for some reason. Have a good night!

Don't Look Back! You're Not Going That Way!—This is one of those particularly fun ones. It assumes you know where you're going. It assumes that life is some clear and linear path with a line from A to B that you just follow. And why would you look back? What part of your past could you possibly learn from? As we all know, Hansel and Gretel didn't leave a trail of crumbs in order to find their way back to safety when they veered off course. They obviously just wanted to fatten up all the fucking gluten-starved forest critters. There are two kinds of people in this world: people who pay attention to their past and try to learn from their mistakes and people who get eaten in the woods. Decide which kind of person you want to be.

ALL OF THOSE ARE BULLSHIT, and I think that's pretty easy to see. But there is one motivational, inspirational quote that is so morally reprehensible that I would like to see it purged from all documents here on Earth to prevent the possibility that one day, when the aliens come down to scour the devastated remains of our scorched wastelands, they stumble upon it. It's a phrase that is so damaging that said aliens (who are probably sad we blew ourselves up before they had a chance to come down here and do it themselves) would use it in their classrooms as the only necessary proof that the human race was simply too stupid to live.

And that phrase is:

Everything Happens for a Reason—I don't know exactly when it happened, but at some point in our lifetimes somebody started saying it, and then other people started saying it, and before long, pretty much everyone had taken this remarkably simplistic repackaging of fate and decided that they believed in it.

What does this ubiquitous phrase mean? If you press people on it for even a few minutes, you'll find that in almost all cases they're not even sure what THEY believe. People who say this have never really stopped and thought about the incredible ramifications of this worldview. Using this thought process as part of your emotional arsenal for dealing with the world is not like adding avocado to a sandwich in the hopes it will be slightly better. It's more like adding a sledgehammer to a sandwich: utterly destructive, rendering the sandwich inedible. It's incompatible with the concept of free will and of human choice. It's antithetical to everything we love about life. BUT people are just so used to saying it that they're willing to let all of those petty details fall by the wayside for the convenience of explaining away the parts of their lives they don't like.

Okay, so if this is your way of saying that you have no input on how your life plays out, that's fine, but then we're pretty much done talking, forever. (Because what's the point in talking? Things are obviously all going according to plan for you so let's just move along!) But if you think you are an active participant in your life,

and more important, if you WOULD LIKE to be an active participant in your life, then you are going to have to take this "Everything
Happens for a Reason" shit and throw it right out the window.

I have a theory as to how this whole thing started and where
it should end. To get there I'll need to start here with some common phrases that are ACTUALLY true and useful:

Life Is Unfair.
Bad Things Happen to Good People.
The Only Sure Things Are Death and Taxes.

Three sentences that are astoundingly less fun than the kinds
of phrases we usually see on Stevie's mug at work. But if you take
a second and think about the life you've lived so far, there is no
question that all three of those things are true.

Life is hard. And explaining why life is unfair and why bad things
happen to good people and why we all die ... well, that's just impossible. It's impossible to look at someone who has just experienced
an unimaginable tragedy and explain it to them. It's impossible to
rationalize why we get only one go-round on this beautiful planet
and something as simple as a tainted burrito bowl or a drunk driver
going the wrong way can end it all. It's impossible.

So we stopped trying.

I guess in some ways people started saying "everything happens for a reason" to help them get through the harder times. It's certainly a lot easier to lie to yourself and pretend that there's some great logic behind the insane randomness that is life. But the reality is that things don't always make sense.

In 2016, there was a small boy visiting the Cincinnati Zoo with his mother. At some point his mother looked up and saw that the boy was gone. He had somehow escaped her watchful eye and had ended up inside the gorilla enclosure. Inside the enclosure there was a seventeen-year-old gorilla named Harambe. Harambe grabbed the child and kind of dragged him around the enclosure willy-nilly. There is some argument here as to what happened next. Some people thought that Harambe was going to kill the child, while others thought that Harambe was protecting the child from the screaming crowd that had gathered around, holding their cell phones and taking videos and frightening the shit out of both the human child and the animal adult.

At that point, the zookeepers shot and killed Harambe. He died a beloved member of the Cincinnati Zoo and a wonderful representative of his species. The child, who was pretty unremarkable (almost all children who are not Mozart are), survived, and will live on and presumably become an adult. The world exploded with outrage and sympathy on both sides. Some people applauded the zoo for valuing human life above profit, while others chided the parent for being irresponsible and allowing her child to claim the life of the primate. But in the end, all pretty much agreed that it was good that the child survived the encounter. And as the world processed this, people began to see the good that could come from this sensational story.

Many would argue that all of this happened for a reason. Those who missed Harambe found solace in the fact that this shed light on the dangerous position animals in captivity are in. Those who were glad the child survived thought it shed necessary light on the lax security measures zoos had in place to protect humans from the wild animals that they'd come to stare at, gape-jawed and chugging Pepsi from giraffe-shaped plastic tumblers.

So, what was the reason? Did the Universe create this incident so people would gain a deeper appreciation for animals? Or did the Universe make sure all of this happened so that zoos made the enclosures more secure? Which one was it?

Or...

Did it just fucking happen? Maybe it just fucking happened. Maybe life happened. Maybe a kid wandered off, as kids do, for no reason. Maybe he fell into the enclosure because of an accident, which often happens, also for no reason. Maybe Harambe grabbed him because animals grab things, often, for no reason, and maybe he got shot and killed and murdered because a bunch of stupid shit happened that doesn't make any sense.

It's easy to poke fun when you're talking about an animal who didn't have much of a life (because he was trapped in a zoo) and a child you don't know (and who nothing really happened to), and to see how ridiculous it is to think that there was some great cosmic force at play that ensured some asshole filmed all of it on an iPhone (vertically, no less).

But how quickly we forget how silly this is when we have to apply the same logic to something we actually care about. When your uncle Phil falls asleep at the wheel of his truck and drives off a bridge and dies, it's much more pleasant to think about what you can learn about the fragility of life. It easy to believe that being reminded of this fragility was the point of his passing rather than learn the lesson that life isn't something you're promised and health isn't something you should expect. But you can't just pick and choose where to apply these kinds of philosophies because they penetrate your soul and become who you are. If you want to be able to make a decision about Harambe, you also need to be able to make a clearheaded decision about Uncle Phil.

And think about how dismissive it is of someone else's life to view their catastrophic demise as a lesson for you to learn. Someone's entire existence boils down to you receiving a lesson that you'll remember for a few days? So maybe Uncle Phil didn't die for a reason (the selfish reason you have now applied to that, which makes his life ALL ABOUT YOU), and maybe you can just be sad because a human life, one that you care about, is over. And maybe you can learn to take something out of it and learn a thing or two on your own that allows you to make sense of the things that happen, but it doesn't mean that it happened *for you*. It's a small distinction, but it's an important one.

When I was twenty-two, my mother was diagnosed with cancer. We went to the doctor's office and the doctor told us that she probably had only six months to live. We asked what kind of cancer it was and he told us that it was a pretty rare type of sarcoma. Incredibly rare, hard to cure, and almost always fast-spreading and fatal. Throughout the diagnosis, I tried to maintain an aura of calm, but on the inside I was totally fucking falling apart. My mother was my rock and now she was going to be gone in less than half a year? A million thoughts were racing through my head, but I can tell you that none of them were "everything happens for a reason."

If I had thought that everything happens for a reason, I would have had to see my mother's eventual death as some sort of learning lesson for me and for my siblings. But that couldn't make any sense, could it? Could there be a legitimate reason that my mother, who'd spent her entire life taking care of three pleasant but definitely undeserving children, would be sentenced to a painful and untimely death? Could there be a legitimate reason that my mother wouldn't live long enough for me to get my act together and to see me do well in life? Could there be a legitimate reason that my mother should die before she became a grandmother, something that I know she would kick ass at?

I'm sorry if this fucks up your worldview, but there was no reason for what was happening to my mom, not one that we mere humans can think of, and there isn't one that we *can't*. And if any of these things happened to your loved ones: I'm sorry. It's terrible. It's miserable. And I wish there was a reason but there isn't. There's just bad luck. There's just the reality that bad things happen to good people. And to bad people. And to boring people.

Some people would say that I would've had more comfort during this diagnosis and prognosis if I believed that everything happened for a reason. And they're probably right. I probably would have felt a lot better.

But feeling better is exactly the OPPOSITE of how I needed to feel. I needed to be miserable and angry and fearful, and most important, I needed to feel desperate. Not better. Desperate.

And so we went on and got a second opinion. That opinion wasn't much more promising. This doctor proposed a disabling amputation along with several other treatments, and he still only thought she would live for another year if she was lucky.

I didn't feel better. I felt more desperate.

And then my mother got lucky, and she was allowed to join a small group of people who were going to be part of a clinical trial for a new chemotherapy intended to treat her precise type of cancer. It wasn't all good news. She would basically have to spend the next year of her life in the hospital. Months and months of chemotherapy, nearly a dozen radiation treatments, and three invasive surgeries were ahead of her. It was to be the worst year of her life. And there was no guarantee that she would get better.

I remember that year well. There was a lot of sleeping on hospital floors. There was a lot of crying and fighting and sadness. She was so sick she could barely stand, and often she couldn't stand on her own for a week or two at a time. The drugs attacked the cancer, but they also attacked her healthy cells and attacked her brain. One of the first pills they gave her to help her deal with the nausea triggered an allergic reaction that almost killed her. On numerous occasions, she would ask me and my sisters to let her stop the treatment and to just let her die. I am positive I would have done the same if I were her.

Being tortured for months on end for an unknown result? I would have quit. I know it. But she didn't. And there's no reason she didn't. She just didn't. She just decided to keep trying and hoped for the best.

And now, eleven years later, she is still here, and she's healthier than ever. And there's no reason for that either. She's just lucky. I'm just lucky.

Although now she calls and texts me ALL THE TIME. So, I mean, well, that's kind of a pain in the ass.

I'm not trying to be a downer by telling you this. What I'm trying to point out is that while thinking that "Everything Happens for a Reason" can often make you feel better, it doesn't actually help anything. People love pulling out this reliable aphorism after something bad has happened, but it makes us passive in life. They should replace this phrase with a more useful one like:

What Can I Learn from This?

That's active. That's exciting. And that's what being alive is all about. Learning and changing as part of your daily life. "Everything happening for a reason" is about how the world affects you. "What can I learn from this?" is about how **you** affect **you**.

And from now on, that's how we are going to approach everything. We're not going to be passive lemmings on this planet, waiting to see what the Universe has in store for us. Because let me tell you, the Universe doesn't care about you. But the good news is, so many people out there are waiting for the Universe to make their wishes come true that if you get out there and take the bull by the horns you'll be one of the only folks making life happen for yourself. There isn't as much competition as you think there is. You're not that great. But neither is anyone else.

pain!

"One could argue that pain is the most universal thing in the human experience."

That's not what you'd expect to hear when you talk to Rachel Bloom, Golden Globe–winning actor and cocreator of *Crazy Ex-Girlfriend*. Rachel is one of the funniest people I know and her show is reshaping how TV networks think about the kinds of shows they can make. But comedy rarely comes out of good times.

"Around the time of my sophomore year in college," Rachel says, "I was nineteen years old and I got involved in something of a love triangle with these two guys who were in my college sketch group. It was partially their fault and partially my fault. I was supposed to be the director of this sketch comedy group and when the shit hit the fan, one of the guys had me removed as director and the other guy (along with everyone else in the group) went along with it. Suddenly, comedy wasn't this pure thing to me anymore."

She was motivated by her "negative" feelings towards this experience. "I'm going to prove them wrong. I'm going to prove they were wrong about me. I'm not going to let them do that. I had anger, revenge fantasy feelings. I'm going to do this thing but also FUCK THEM!"

Unfortunately, it's not always as easy as that. "When I got one of my first writing jobs, one of those same guys was on the staff. I was the only girl and I was the youngest. Although my ex wasn't mean to me, some of the other guys were, and the whole thing made me feel ganged up on by a group of men all over again. I would go home every day and cry." That's when Rachel says she "got really good as a comedy writer. The work that came out of that period was so emotional. Feeling pathetic, feeling emotional disenfranchisement. Feeling powerless and ganged up on gave me vulnerability through anger. Fuck you, and fuck you through the tears."

But feeling vulnerable wasn't enough for Rachel to thrive. She also needed to take those feelings and use them. Back in the day, Rachel used to tell herself that "everything happens for a reason." But as she grew wiser, that mind-set changed. "Once I stopped thinking the mystical *something* is watching over me...It's not meant to be. There's no such thing as fate. I'm in charge of my fate."

And to be in charge of your fate you have to concede your flaws, Rachel explains. "Everything happens for a reason is a warm cushion. To actually admit responsibility for your actions and to admit that you're an idiot and you actually fucked up, that's really scary. To take in that damage is a lot harder than just saying everything happens for a reason."

chapter four

how to hate yourself
completely
without really trying

The engine that drove me for forty-two years of my life was self-hatred and competition, anger, loneliness, wanting to be heard and wanting to be understood...Now I'm putting a lot of obsessive energy into not doing that because I think it's going to kill me. It's like metal on metal, grinding out all the joy...But I'm not sure I would have had the motivation I needed to tour, and to drive around the country... alone...for fifteen years...if I didn't have those things.

—Matt Nathanson (singer-songwriter)

Have you ever heard the story of Icarus? I'll keep it brief, but here's the gist:

Icarus was the son of a super important Greek craftsman back in the time when everything was Greek. But due to some unfortunate circumstances, he was captive in a bad place. Icarus is actually like a lot of us. Stuck in a bad job or a bad apartment or a bad city or a bad relationship. In his case, Icarus was trapped in the labyrinth that his father had created on Crete. This too is not that different from most of us, who are still paying for some of the shitty things our parents did when we were kids.

Icarus's father gave him wax and a set of wings and told him to flap his arms and fly away. Sure, it wasn't a perfect plan, but at least he was trying. Before he got up into the air, Icarus's daddy told him to not fly too low (to which Icarus responded by rolling his eyes and being like, "Yeah, no shit, Dad") but also warned him not to fly too close to the sun because the heat from the sun would melt the wax and destroy the wings. This was actually super important advice, the kind a modern dad rarely gives.

So Icarus started flapping and flapping and suddenly he was up and flying and he was out of the labyrinth and freedom was definitely in his sights. But here Icarus made a tragic error: he started feeling really good about himself. A lot of people call it hubris, but you can call it cockiness or self-love or anything you want.

The point is that Icarus forgot the practicalities of life. He forgot everything he had been taught about physics and heat and wax and safety and he just felt really super cool, like a sixteen-year-old borrowing his uncle's sports car for the first time. And much like a new driver behind the wheel of a vintage Camaro, Icarus just thought he was too damn awesome to be careful.

Needless to say, it wasn't long before his wings started melting. He was still flapping his arms, though, because his ego had basically detached from his reality. Shortly thereafter, Icarus fell into the sea and drowned to death.

If Icarus had only kept his wits about him and been aware of his limitations, he would have survived and maybe even become more like the successful godlike figurehead his ego had convinced him he was. Maybe he would have become a super cool Greek figure like Zeus or Achilles. But instead, he just died in the water like a little idiot and is only remembered for being kind of a smug asshole.

So, don't be like Icarus. This chapter is all about accepting and acknowledging your limitations. It's not fun to be told you can't fly close to the sun, but maybe it's the only thing that's going to keep your self-important ass alive.

Okay, everyone. It's honesty time. Much like getting a colonoscopy, this is going to be a little uncomfortable at first, but it's actually really important, and it just might save your life. So if this feels like a little bit of a pain in your ass, that means things are going well.

If you're the average person, you're probably convinced that you like yourself. Moreover, you're probably convinced that it's important that you like yourself. Liking yourself is a source of confidence and it teaches other people around you that you are worthy of being liked, right?

WRONG. Liking yourself is a one-way ticket on Oceanic Airlines where you will eventually disappear and become one with the giant and vast blue sea.

But here's the good news. Even through all the endless positive reinforcement you've gotten your whole life, there's a little smart voice inside you that knows that you don't really like yourself THAT much. I mean, you're fine. You're not a total piece of shit. But you're not that great.

Before we go any further, I have a little assignment for you.

Close your eyes and imagine the perfect person (but not in like a sex doll way, more like a Build-A-Bear way). Like, everything you would want to be. Top to bottom. There are no right answers here. You don't need to admit any of this to anyone. Just be honest and write it down. I want you to take out a piece of paper and answer the following questions:

○ What does this person look like? Height? Weight? Eye color? Hair color? Build?

Where does this person live? What is their home like? What do they do for a living? What do they do in their free time?

○ How much money do they make per year? How much time do they contribute to others? How much money do they raise for charity?

How much do they contribute to society as a whole?
○ How do they make the world a better place for everyone?

How would their best friends describe them? How would a stranger describe them?

What will their tombstone say? What will their legacy be?

Now, everyone's definition of "great" is different. Look at what you've written down. If you've been honest, you have a pretty good approximation of what "great" is to you.

How close are you to this person? How similar is your life to the life you described above in this very moment? I'm going to guess that the answer is "not very."

I'm proud of you. You've set nearly impossible standards for yourself. How could you possibly live up to the things you said about this perfect person? What are you, some kind of Greek god? Well, of course not. You shouldn't feel bad about not being perfect. You should feel normal, because NO ONE is that great. Except for maybe Bill and Melinda Gates. But you're not the nerdy founder of Microsoft and his philanthropic wife. You're just a person. And that's okay. Take a deep breath. This isn't that big a deal. You're not that great. Just like everyone else.

See, the problem is that you've been too easy on yourself. Your standards of excellence are very high, but for some reason you have much lower standards for yourself. You've done this as a method of self-protection. You don't like feeling bad and other people have told you that feeling bad is bad for you, so you've set up this really clever defense mechanism. Rather than constantly challenging yourself to be better, you've felt better about the fact that you are worse.

Now it's time to knock that shit off.

I'm not trying to get you to be all depressed and fucked up beyond recognition. I'm telling you all this because REALLY, YOU CAN BE BETTER. You probably still won't be GREAT, nor should you expect to be, but you can IMPROVE. But first you really have to come to terms with the fact that you're not. At least, not yet.

A caterpillar doesn't sit around in a dark bedroom surrounded by empty ice cream cartons because it's depressed that it isn't a butterfly yet. But a caterpillar also isn't satisfied as a caterpillar. A caterpillar is an eating machine and spends all of its time, LITERALLY all of its time, trying to not be a caterpillar anymore. The caterpillar knows that being something better is out there for it. The caterpillar knows that it could spend its life eating leaves and occasionally his friends (yes, sometimes they're cannibals, just like us), or it could spend every waking hour trying to become a beautiful, elegant, majestic monarch butterfly. To glide, to soar, to go up and down and around and to never stand still for pictures when people try to take them. That's the life!

So don't be sad that you're a larva. You're supposed to be a larva. Only by being fully accepting of your larva-ness will you have any chance to figure out what it takes to get your ass into a chrysalis and turn into a much better form of yourself. And by the way, caterpillars only have like a month from birth to death to get their act together. You've had DECADES, so you better get your shit together now and count your lucky stars that no one has eaten you yet...

(And by the way, you WANT to become a butterfly. But there's a chance you'll become a moth and be stuck eating people's gross old sweaters for all eternity. If you fail at being a butterfly, you become a gross, gross, disgusting moth that nobody loves. No pressure.)

but i'm not all bad, am i?

Not to jump from one metaphor right into the next, but try to imagine yourself on a boat. Suddenly, the boat starts to fill up with water. What do you do? Do you just casually stroll around the boat pointing out all the parts of the boat that don't have leaks in them? Or do you run wildly around, trying to identify and fix leaks? No one cares if 80 percent of the boat is still float-ing, because the water will just keep lapping in, and soon it will be 70 percent. And then 60 percent. And all of a sudden there's a movie about the boat and it's almost four hours long and Leo-nardo DiCaprio dies even though there is definitely enough room on the door.

As you may have guessed, you're the boat.

So, take a deep breath, stop congratulating yourself on all the things that aren't wrong with you, and start looking to plug up all of your holes. (I didn't mean this sexually, but it came out that way the first time and I'm keeping it here because it made me laugh. I'm not sorry.)

Dig down deep here and try to be honest because you can only fix problems that you're aware of.

what do you not like about you?

I'll lead by example here. And I'm going to be frank. First and foremost, there are some things I cannot change. I am 5'8" with shoes on. I have a very slow metabolism, so no matter how much I try I am always slowly gaining weight. There's nothing wrong with being short OR fat, but I personally don't like those things about me. I also have a kind of annoying body. It collects fat in all the wrong places, like under my arms and around my waist, so I have this weird-looking muffin top that is so soft it even appears when I'm just wearing underwear. I also have caveman teeth. I have an occluded bite, so I look like I'm two steps back in the evolutionary process, but unlike those man-apes, I'm totally incapable of caring for myself. I can barely start a fire with a lighter and a bunch of newspaper, much less two rocks and a twig. I really don't like how I look and there really isn't a whole lot I can do about that. I can only choose to be with people who like how I look, which as a result of my own insecurities will always make me question their judgment. Thankfully not everyone is as shallow as me.

So those are some things I can't change. At least, not in any real way.

I'm easily distracted. I get scared a lot, and easily—by horror films and roller coasters. I crave attention. When I'm thinking something, I have to express it or I burst. People who have me in their lives are subjected to my nonsense all the damn time. I have made very many bad decisions in relationships. Decisions that have severely negatively impacted me and others around me. I've never done something truly stupid like cheat on someone, but I've stayed in relationships for too long. Sometimes it was too long because the other person was unhappy and I knew it, but I held on for dear life because I was afraid of being left. Sometimes it was too long because I knew that it was going to end eventually, but I was too afraid that I'd never find anyone else who loved me again. I've romanticized relationships too, making them mean more to me than anything else even though they're just things that change and evolve like everything else in life. I stood on top of a roof and thought about killing myself. I thought about killing myself a lot. I went to a lot of therapy. There's nothing really weird about having moments in which you want to kill yourself, but I'm embarrassed for my own reasons. My reasons were all about fear and self-pity instead of pain or despair.

That seems like a lot. But there's more.

I am totally emotional. While I'm glad I'm not dead inside, I am overly sensitive. I remember every single mean thing every person has ever said to me. Do you ever think back to that thing you said in high school that was a little mean and then you reach out to that person on Facebook and apologize, and they're like, "Hey, thanks for reaching out but honestly I don't remember that at all, all I remember is that time you choked on your Go-Gurt in the cafeteria and vomited everywhere"? Except if you said it to me I would be like, "Yes, I remember it. I remember it well and it was so destructive that it actually ruined one of my best relationships. She said something ten years later that triggered an emotional response in me and I walked out of the apartment we'd lived in together for three years and then called her to break up with her because I was too humiliated to face the fact that your comment about my gross face in the ninth grade led me to have such an astonishing mental breakdown." So yeah, I'm a little too sensitive. What else?

Oh, yeah, did I mention I'm insecure? Did I mention that because I don't consider myself good-looking, strong, or particularly charming, I've spent my whole life trying to become other things that might be attractive to people around me? I've tried to read a lot, so I can sound smarter than I am. I've tried to hone a sense of humor, so I can make people laugh and trick them into thinking they're having a good time around me. And I think most people who meet me would say that I'm either smart or funny or both (if they say I'm handsome, you shouldn't trust any-thing they say because my head looks like a pineapple got fucked by a baboon), but every day I walk around scared, waiting for people to find out that in reality I'm not that smart and not that funny. I mean, I'm not an unfunny idiot. But I meet people ALL THE TIME whom I consider MUCH funnier and MUCH smarter and MUCH more charming than I am. And I think about all the people in my life who like being around me and I wonder if they know the secret that I know: that there are other people out there who are simply better and more interesting than me, and I am sure that they're only in my life because they haven't randomly bumped into those other people yet. That is the only reason that makes any sense to me.

I am insecure and shallow and afraid and weak and ugly. I am sometimes unkind to people who don't deserve it. I am impatient with my family (even though they only deserve it half the time). I am simply not that great.

And I am just like everyone else. I don't have to be scared of any of that. I don't have to be embarrassed about any of that. In fact, the fact that I know all of those things and am not ashamed to say them out loud is maybe the best thing about me.

I am armed. I am equipped. Take a look at your own list. I hope it's as diverse and full of problems as mine.

You need to know that every single time you make a decision you carry all of that baggage with you. You may be able to juggle a few thoughts at a time, but at every moment, your brain is spitting out millions of hypothetical outcomes to every single decision that's ahead of you. All of those visuals, hurtling at you and hitting you in the face, are all colored with all the baggage you've collected since the day you were born. There's nothing you can do about that, BUT...

Once you know what your baggage is, you can take it into account. The rest of your life is going to be based on what decisions you make from this moment on. So you need to know who you are. You need to deal with it. And you need to learn to love it (not because it is perfect, but because it is imperfect), to hold yourself close and to embrace yourself.

You already have everything you need inside of yourself to become better. You don't need to buy a pamphlet or an activated charcoal lemonade juice cleanse. You don't need a yoga roller and acupuncture needles all over your taint. Your insecurities are right here with you. And they will make you strong.

We've been told, for some unknown fucking reason, that insecurities are bad things. It's the opposite. Here's some really quick proof. Take a good look at someone who doesn't seem to have any insecurities. Take a look at someone who never says they're wrong and never apologizes. Take a look at someone who thinks they're perfect. I'll tell you what you're looking at: a total fucking asshole. This is a person who never thought they needed to improve. If you're never sorry, you never learn how to not make mistakes. If you're never wrong, you don't have any reason to learn how to be right. The world is changing every moment. There are seven billion of us, with hundreds of thousands being born and dying every day. If you think you've got this whole "being alive" thing figured out, you are most assuredly 100 percent a total narcissistic, psychotic piece of shit, and if you're a guy you probably also have a really small dick, well, just because.

So don't agonize about your insecurities. Reach deep inside of yourself, pull them out, put them on the couch next to you, and look at them and say, "Thank you." These are the things that are going to give you the power to have the life you want (more or less). If you haven't gotten to all of them, keep going. Like gluten allergies, a lot of these insecurities can appear for the first time in adulthood, and it's your daily job to track them and expose them, and then benefit from them.

You are your insecurities. If that doesn't make you happy, well, good, because no one gives a shit if you're happy.

agony!

Jon Ronson has been a best-selling author and a successful filmmaker for the last fifteen years (though he's been prolific and relevant much longer than that). But if you ask Jon Ronson what he's going to do next he will tell you he's not sure. "I think there'll always be something to keep me going. I'm not entirely sure what." To young writers out there, I think it's important to know that this kind of thinking isn't just for those without success. Uncertainty about the future lingers on, well, forever.

And happiness and certainty aren't a key component of what makes a writer a writer, if you ask Jon Ronson: "We do this because we're fucked up and we want to fill a psychological hole. It all comes from the kind of scream of anxiety. I wake up in the morning and it's anxiety that propels me to be my best, to write." If it's all anxiety, though, why choose it? "You do it because the alternative is so much worse. I would stumble out of my office at the end of the day, feeling that my brain had been sandpapered. Physical pain is one thing but what is worse is the sort of scream of failure."

"If it's easy," Jon says, "it's not going to be good work. It should be hard. It should be agony. That fact that it's agony means you're a proper writer. You need self-belief and self-hatred, weird other things too. There's nothing sane about the belief that you're a total failure even after a lifetime of success."

So why keep doing it? "It's not out of virtue. It's out of anxiety. It's how I stop the screaming."

Jon Ronson is a hero not because he does things with ease but because he does what he himself considers nearly impossible.

chapter five

say goodbye to happiness

Whenever you feel anxious, remind yourself that life is a pointless game and nothing you do matters.

—Isaac Marion (author)

everyone is either wrong or a liar

If you ask people what they want, they will often tell you what isn't important to them. They'll tell you that they don't really care about success. They'll tell you that making money isn't something they even really think about all that much. They'll tell you that fame and fortune and fabulous living aren't important to them, and that all they care about is just "being happy." If you ask them what they mean by "happy" they'll usually describe something really simple and attainable.

Let's try it:

Hey, friend. What do you really want in life?

What do I want? Oh, not much really. I just want someone to love. They don't need to be rich or beautiful or fabulous or popular or anything like that. I mean, I'm not crazy. I don't need to have the best person. I just need a person who is kind and who looks at me with love and admiration.

Wait. So you don't want that person to be great?

Oh, no, of course they'll be great. But not in the usual way. They don't need to be brilliant or the best at anything or all that confident. They just need to love me.

Don't you think you're kind of setting the bar pretty low? I mean, your dog loves you . . .

I'm just being realistic. We can't all have the best of everything, can we?

Well, you certainly fucking can't, especially not with that shitty attitude. How about more material things, like a house? Do you want a nice house?

Oh, sure, sure, of course I do. Nothing fancy. I don't need anything fancy! Nothing super luxurious or large. Just a nice simple place that I can call home.

That doesn't even make any sense. You can do that right now with anyplace on Earth. How is that a good representation of the thing you WANT?

Some people need fancy things like running water and warmed towels, but not me. I just want a lovely porch with a rocking chair and a bird feeder where the blue jays feel comfortable stopping by in the spring to sing me their songs.

You can go live in the fucking woods, right now, for free. Just be a hermit and build your rocking chair with twigs and leaves. You don't even need a job for that. Is there even a job you truly want?

Of course there is. Of course. I really want a job that is steady and dependable. I'm not one of those crazy weirdos who needs to be "intellectually challenged" or "creatively stimulated," you know? That's a bunch of horsepucky. I just need a nice nine to five that helps me pay the bills on time and gives me two weeks a year off to really work on my golf swing.

You don't have that already?

Well, haha, I guess I do! I guess I already have all the things I want hahahahaha. No need for me to work hard to get anything else I am very fulfilled hahahaha what do you mean I look crazy just because I am laughing hysterically and definitely not angry or defensive at all? Hahahahaha.

Soooooooooo, basically, if you ask people what they want, they will look you in the eye and they will lie to you, and they will tell you that they aspire to mediocrity. (If they're not lying, they're just incredibly stupid and I DO NOT KNOW which one is worse.)

Now, before you get all high-and-mighty and feel like I'm dismissing these simple things, I'm not. A person to love and a nice place to call home and a steady job are nothing to be sneezed at. We should all be so lucky as to have those things. They are great and important and potentially attainable if you're lucky **and** work hard, and while they're all things we should gladly settle and be grateful for, they're probably not the things you dreamed about when you envisioned what your life was going to be.

Why can't you have both? Why can't you have the simple things but also have (or at least give yourself the option to have) everything else?

Of course, the examples I'm using are obviously skewed around fame and fortune, but that's just because those are easily digestible concepts. Everyone out there has their own set of desires and ideals. Fame and fortune would probably NOT be what most people want. But within each person's individual framework, based on where they live and what they consider important, there is SOMETHING aspirational to strive for. Everyone has seen their own shooting star and knows what it looks like. I'm really not telling you to want what I want, or what anyone else wants. I'm telling you to reach for the thing that would mean the most to YOU that is ALSO the hardest to reach.

Now, take a step back and think about what you WANT, not what you think you CAN GET.

People have been trained to not think about, to not admit, and certainly to not fucking go after what they really want. THAT would lead to nothing but disappointment, right?

Everyone wants the best life partner for them. Everyone wants the most beautiful place they can imagine to call home. Everyone wants a fulfilling creative job that challenges them and makes them feel like they're living those forty hours a week to the full-est. But everyone is afraid to say it because they feel like they don't have a chance to get it. And they're probably right.

It's a lot easier to throw a stone at the ground and expect to make contact than it is to throw a stone at a fast-flying bird and expect to hit it. But when you think about it, whether you throw the stone at a passing seagull or right down to the ground, that rock is eventually going to settle in the same place. The journey is just different.

Not to draw too grim of a comparison, but take a second and remind yourself that you are going to be dead pretty soon. It could be tomorrow or in sixty years, but in the grand scheme of things, you're going to be dead and gone and buried in the near future. The same goes for your doctor, your mailman, and the guy who made your mocha-choca-latte with extra whipped car-amel this morning. They're all either going to get burned and placed into canisters or shoved into an uncomfortable box and buried in the ground—and pretty soon.

We're all going to the same place. So isn't it worth taking a good shot at the bird in the sky before you end up in the ground instead of just resigning yourself to the ground right now?

Here's the bad news. You and everyone else around you have been trained not to just settle for mediocrity, but to actually strive for it. You've been force-fed the concept that simple is better, that average is supreme, that losing is winning. You've been running towards the wrong goal and you've wasted a tremendous amount of your precious life trying to go after something that you've incorrectly convinced yourself you want. Honestly, you're a fucking idiot.

You don't want a fine, good, average life. You want a nonstop roller-coaster incredible life full of adventure and fear and joy and love and hate and ups and downs and you want to be able to have everything you ever wanted. That's what you want.

And if you take a really good crack at it, and you fail, you'll STILL just have an average life just like everyone else.

If you go through life like you actually want something, the worst thing that can possibly happen to you is that you'll end up with the thing that everyone else is pretending to want.

Most people can't deal with this. Their brains are so tainted and their wills are so crushed that they must instinctively fight against this kind of thinking. If right now you find yourself defending the idea that you want a nice, normal, nothing life, then go ahead and put this book down. You'll get exactly that, and the emotional terrorists will have won. Get back to us when you're lying on your deathbed wishing you'd ever done anything worth remembering. Or actually don't; we'll be too busy to listen to that whiny, complain-y nonsense.

Okay, so that's the bad news. Here's the good news:

One of the reasons everyone is so afraid to go after anything worthwhile is because most things in life that are worth getting are really, really, really hard to get. The girl you want, the guy you want, the job you want, the car you want, the house you want, the life you want...well, it's not going to be easy to get. Those things are rare. You probably won't get them. EVERYONE probably won't get them. The person who will somehow defy all odds and get the thing that they really want is going to be the person who wants it the most and works the hardest for it.

make that person be you

Oh, did that seem like more bad news? Well, it's not, and here's why. Almost everyone you meet is still running, screaming wildly, towards mediocrity. There's a huge-ass mob of scared idiots cluttering up the middle, which means there's actually a ton of room at the top. There's so much room at the top, actually, that people who are aiming at mediocrity are occasionally just falling ass backward into success! Imagine if they were trying even a little bit. Imagine if you were. Imagine if you just actually went after the things you actually wanted.

A word of caution: there's one small side effect to going after the things you want. If for some reason you decide that the thing you want is to *be happy*, it's probably not going to happen.

if you want to be happy you're an idiot

Before we get into how to try to actually be "happy," let's take a moment to discuss how stupid that actually is. I mean, really, how have we become so totally insane as a people that we allow ourselves to discuss "happiness" as life's ultimate goal? What an insane and impossible objective to set. What a total and blatant disregard of what life is.

Happiness is an emotion. That's it. That's all it is. It's ONE emotion. It is one of many emotions we humans are wired to feel. Yet somehow, somewhere along the way, someone convinced everyone that it's the only emotion that matters. Somehow, people became convinced that the other emotions are just distractions from the one emotion that we consider the most pleasant.

But really, emotions are responses to the things that happen in your life and the way you understand them in your brain. Some emotions are enjoyable and some emotions are not, but they're ALL your only way to really understand any part of the world in which you live. Your emotions are designed to help you figure out your life, by repeating actions that lead to emotions that are transformative and productive, and by avoiding actions that lead to discontent and dissatisfaction. Your job as a human is to perform ACTIONS (because those are what actually make up your very limited time here on this funky-ass planet) and to allow yourself to feel the natural emotional responses that come from those actions.

This starts when you are very, very young. When you're a child, you are an idiot. But you are still capable of ACTION, and those actions led to emotions and those emotions led to learning and advancement. Think of the first time you got caught lying. You lied because it either got you out of a predicament or because it caused you immediate pleasure, but because you were a child (and therefore an idiot), you got caught, and you got into trouble, and then you had a new emotion or two: maybe fear, maybe shame, maybe guilt, maybe something else entirely, maybe a combination of all of those things. And those emotions dictated your actions moving forward. Next time, before you lied, you probably weighed that decision differently. Rather than looking at the lie in a vacuum, you asked yourself (without even knowing it), "Is the immediate ease of telling this lie equal to, better than, or worse than the eventual shame, guilt, or fear that I will feel if the lie is discovered?" Lying became more difficult once you'd learned to attach an emotional gravity to it. This is one of the ways in which you became moral. This is one of the ways in which you learned to be a human, by passively feeling the emotions that were at work inside of you while you performed actions. To this day, that is how you learn and that is how you grow and that is how you become less shitty. Allowing yourself to feel the full weight and severity of all your actions is what makes you the person that you are.

But fuck that, right?

Let's all just decide to pretend we're happy all the fucking time. Let's just only focus on THAT ONE EMOTION.

One emotion does not a human make. Whether you believe we were created and beautifully designed or you believe we are all just strange-looking accidental meatsacks, there is no question that we have the capacity, and perhaps even the responsibility, to feel an unbelievably wide range of emotions. Happiness, sadness, joy, fear, anger, rage, bliss, grief, excitement, regret, anxiety, lust, nervousness, desire . . . These are all parts of the human experience and they exist for very specific reasons.

Rage allows us to act aggressively towards things to protect ourselves or the ones we love. Regret allows us to reflect upon what has gone wrong or badly and hopefully learn from those decisions. Fear allows us to measure the danger around us and act in a way that ensures our survival. Desire allows us to buck complacency and aim to better our lives. Lust allows us to fuck things.

But apparently those are all "negative" feelings that we should set aside and we should all just sit around feeling good and smiling like we just woke up from anesthesia after getting our wisdom teeth removed.

People use "happy" as a goal because they are afraid of what life really is. People who want to be "happy" don't actually get to feel "happy," because they don't actually ever get to feel ANY-THING. So next time you meet someone who is "happy," ask them to explain exactly what the fuck is wrong with them. Maybe the emotion they feel after that will be an authentic one.

make a very stupid list

Now that we know that the things you've said you wanted aren't just mediocre and stupid but also impossible, it's time for us to refocus and figure out how to actually take at least one meager step in the direction of building a life that is worth living and isn't just sixty-some years of wasting oxygen and adding to landfills with your empty Hot Pocket wrappers and expired unused condoms.

You've already wasted so much of your life at this point, it's important that we try to simplify our quest. So let's divide all the things in the world into two categories: Superficial Things and Supernatural Things. Superficial Things are the ones you can buy and Supernatural Things are the ones you can't. Let's begin:

superficial things

Here you should make a list of the tangible things that you want. These are not deep or meaningful concepts like love or joy or any bullshit garbage like that. This is where you make a list of material goods you want to possess. Cars, houses, diamonds, the world's largest inflatable giraffe, a pool full of hard-bodied male models covered in sesame oil. Whatever. Write it down and make it honest. If something feels really horrifying to put in writing and you're embarrassed to admit you want it, then you're doing this right. I'll give you some examples:

○
- Giant beautiful house made out of marble and glass on a hillside somewhere
- A different car for every day of the week
- Expensive watches
- A bunch of iPhones so when I drop one and it cracks, I don't give a shit, I just throw it away
○
- Gold-plated cocker spaniel
- An entire refrigerator dedicated specifically to bacon
- A waterslide, but with champagne
○
- That one pair of shoes that looks like every other pair of shoes but for some reason costs three thousand dollars

supernatural things

Next you should make a list of the intangible things you want. Dream big. Do you want someone who loves you? Or is that just the beginning? Maybe you want someone who loves you so fucking much that they have a hard time breathing at the very thought of losing you. Do you want someone nice and sweet? Or are those obvious? Maybe you want someone who lights a fire inside you. Maybe you want someone who you think is totally out of your league and that person makes you constantly strive to be better, each and every minute of each and every day, because you can't stand the idea of them being with anyone as imperfect as you, and this deep desire compels you to constantly press forward in life, becoming better and better in a never-ending quest to feel deserving of the love you so deeply want. Or maybe you just want someone nice, you stupid asshole.

- O A job that doesn't feel like a job—a job that makes you want to get up in the morning and sprint out the door because you long for the fulfillment you get at work
- O A sense of knowing your place in the world and an accepting of your many great attributes and an equally important understanding of your flaws
- O A lover and companion you consider godlike
- The sex drive of a hormonal panther

Now take a moment and really look at the above lists. Have the steps you've been taking so far in life led you down the path towards these goals? Have your choices brought you closer to these nearly impossible desires? Or are you just consistently running on a log in a river like an old cartoon, expending a whole shitload of energy without ever really going anywhere? It's probably the latter and you're just using everything you have in you to stay above water. Well, the good news is, you've already accomplished mediocrity with every moment of your shitty little life, and it's time to jump off that log and hop onto solid ground.

Of course your inner Boring Loser Self is thinking, "We can't all have a giant house made of marble with a champagne waterslide." And your inner Boring Loser Self is right, but if you set your eyes on a marble house with a slide of bubbly and you fall short, you may just fail and end up with a really nice house you love with a regular waterslide. So, I guess your failure isn't too bad after all. But if you keep aiming for that mediocre shed in the woods to begin with and you fail at that, you're going to end up living in a tent, eating the scraps that campers leave behind and shitting into an old can on the side of a polluted pond.

This is your chance to escape the cage of "happiness." This is your time to start living and to stop lying to yourself. If you stop caring about your happiness you might actually have a chance to perform some actions in an attempt to reach your actual goals. If that happens, you might wake up one day and discover a bright and exhilarating feeling coming from inside of you. Maybe it will be a tiny burst of happiness. And if you don't recognize that feeling, it's because you haven't actually felt that emotion since you were a little idiot child.

Never forget: you're probably going to fail anyway, so you might as well go for gold. After all, you don't want to live with regret. Or do you?

reminder: you could die at literally
almost any moment

rage!

"I grew up pretty angry. I had a lot of angst. I've always rooted my identity in being this angsty teenager and I haven't grown out of it. I'm thirty-six."

Before Bobby Kim (aka Bobby Hundreds) became one of the most innovative artists in men's apparel, he was just like everybody else. "I'm a minority. A second-generation Korean immigrant, and I was a middle child: a minority on top of being a minority." Bobby felt invisible at best and dismissed at worst. Where did he find the energy to start one of the most recognizable lifestyle brands in the world?

"I felt like I was never heard. I wasn't getting the attention I sought from my parents or teachers or girls and it made me really angry. I felt like I didn't fit in. There was no future for what I wanted to do." Bobby was a Korean kid in Riverside with a blog. "There was no future. It was just old, white, rich guys from Orange County and I'm not that. My parents drilled that into my head too. They immigrated here so I could get a 'real' job."

Growing up, "there were a lot of things to be pissed off about. I had daddy issues. My dad and I didn't have the warmest relationship growing up. It gave me a deep desire to impress other dudes. Male subcultures are about winning the attention and respect of other men."

If Bobby's relationship with his father hadn't been strained, he might not have found it in himself to find his passion. "Everything isn't happy and perfect," he says, "and ignoring your anger is dismissive. I'm a pretty passionate person. Anger is my most powerful emotion. It doesn't have to be a destructive or corrosive force. I've been able to use it in a way that gives me the drive and energy to see that there are problems in the world that we need to fix. Anger is just passion. Anger is a gift.

"Every happy person I know is incredibly boring. They're solid people that you can rely on, but I want to affect and change the world. I want you to feel my impact."

chapter six

the dangers of thinking you're great

Whenever I'm starting to feel too confident or good about myself I like to play a recording of my own speaking voice. Unless you're Scarlett Johansson, nothing takes you back to zero faster than hearing what your voice actually sounds like.

—Jennifer Kaytin Robinson (writer)

At this point you may still be thinking, "I actually do think I'm pretty great. What's wrong with that? I'm not hurting anyone!"

Wrong. You are. You're hurting yourself and you're hurting everyone around you. Your endless stream of self-love makes you completely unbearable to be around and your satisfaction makes you stagnant and useless. Life is a rushing river with refreshing water and endless twists and turns. But right now you're a dirty lake full of brain-eating amoebas and dead fish.

I know you're not convinced. I know there's a part of you that feels like the confidence you get from thinking you're better than you are makes you happier and more pleasant to be around and motivated to get out of bed and face the day each morning with all the energy of a Jack Russell terrier that just drank a bucket of espresso. But while you might think you're taking on the world, you're actually just barking up the wrong tree and peeing on your own feet in the mud.

The number one problem that results from thinking you're great is that you gravely miscalculate what you deserve. As a result, you end up giving up or, even worse, getting desperate and *settling*.

Let's take a second and think about unicorns. Unicorns are fucking delightful. You've never seen or even heard of a unicorn that wasn't glorious. Long, sturdy legs and rippling lean muscles under a perfect and silky coat. Sometimes they can fly. Sometimes they can talk. They obviously have a pretty legit glam squad because they turn and whip their manes around and a record scratches and the party stops like Beyoncé just walked into the room.

Seemingly, there is nothing at all wrong with unicorns. They are perfect beings.

Oh, except for one thing: they don't fucking exist.

When you think you're great, you spend your time looking for unicorns. You think you're pretty damn special and that you deserve the very best. In fact, you believe that you deserve perfection. You think you deserve a unicorn.

This causes two problems. The obvious one is that you're wandering around like an idiot looking for a mythical creature. The less obvious one is that you have delegitimized and devalued the things in your world that are good and are worth desiring.

Because you know what a unicorn is? A unicorn is just a horse with a cone-shaped tumor on its head. As you wander the prairies searching for the elusive unicorn, you literally just walked by a million unbelievable horses and missed your shot with those horses (and as a bonus, you made the horses feel like shit about themselves). All the things that make unicorns cool are also present in horses, except for the useless horn (unless, that is, you're trying to get your unicorn to impale someone or you have a thing for VERY painful sex).

And there you are, turning your nose up at horses. Who the fuck are *you*? You're god's gift to equines? Any of these horses could have let you walk behind them and kicked you in the head and shattered your skull if they wanted to, but they didn't, because you're not worth their time (and it's not easy to get human blood-stains off of horseshoes . . . Trust me, I've tried).

The point is that you should always aim high. You should always try to reach for the stars. But you should also know that you're not going to get anywhere near the stars unless you're an astronaut. So, this leaves you with two options:

1. Be reasonable about your desires
2. Become an astronaut and reach for the stars

Option 1 is perfect for you if you want to have a boring-ass life (see Chapter Five). But if you want Option 2, you're going to have to become an astronaut. Now, obviously I don't mean a literal astronaut. I mean that you're going to work hard, train every day of your life, and commit yourself to becoming the best, mentally and physically, so you can reach the top of the heap. Last time they were looking for astronauts, roughly eighteen thousand applied for less than ten spots. Just ask Mike Massimino, retired astronaut and author of *Spaceman*, who will tell you that "the most difficult aspect of being an astronaut is being selected to be an astronaut. Thousands apply and only a few are picked. Sticking out from the crowd among stiff competition is hard to do. Those who are picked are extremely fortunate."

But if you find a way to make it to space, all that work pays off. "There's something incredibly rewarding about space exploration— partly because it helps provide context for what it means to be alive on this planet floating in space but also because we're always looking to do things that haven't been done before—to push the envelope of what is possible."

See? It can be done. Mike is an example. He wanted the stars so he went out there and got them.

But if you've decided that you're going to go for Option 2, you're going to have to be willing to learn and grow, and the better you think you are, the less likely you are to do any of that.

As you take steps towards improving, you will realize that there are two things in life that are pretty much certain:

Smart People Know They're Dumb
Dumb People Think They're Smart

Do you remember when you were a teenager and you thought you knew everything? Do you remember stomping up to your room and being really mad because you thought you had it all figured out and all the adults were just wasting your time trying to *teach you anything*?

Remember when you fell in love for the first time and you were 100 percent sure that this was the only love you were going to feel? Remember when you had your first real breakup and you were sure you were never going to recover? Remember how you were never going to love again?

Do you remember knowing it all?

And then do you remember when you finally really became an adult, and you looked back at how you used to think you knew everything? And you realized what a total idiot you were?

You can't *believe* how dumb your teenage self was. There was so little you knew about life, and yet you were so confident in your myopic worldview and shortsightedness.

That's a great lesson. That's a really important moment for most people. The day that you realize you have a lot of learning to do and a lot of growing up to do is the day you really start becoming not a total idiot for the first time.

Then something terrible happened. You forgot to keep realizing that the things that made you think you knew everything the first time are still inside you, festering and multiplying like bacteria in old yogurt. In your twenties and maybe again in your thirties and in some cases all the way up to your seventies you decided that **this time** you were right about the way the world works.

Twenties you: "I know I was wrong about who I was going to love forever when I was in my teens, but now I know for sure! There is no way this relationship can go wrong and destroy me and send me to therapy for years!"

Thirties you: "Oh, man, I was so stupid in my twenties. Thank god I finally figured out relationships. I was so dumb before, but now I understand everything! The chances of me getting my heart broken again are zero!"

Seventies you: "Well, I've had three divorces and none of my grandchildren visit me. I guess I've definitely got it all figured out this time and I should marry my young nurse and there is absolutely no way she will kill me and clean out my estate!"

MASSIVE EYE ROLL, Y'ALL.

The only thing you've ever been right about 100 percent of the time in your life is that you were wrong about the world, but as you get older there's this bizarre pressure to "grow up" and forget that lesson.

Growing up is great and important and requires doing the single hardest thing that human beings ever have to do: take responsibility. But for some reason we pair "growing up" with the idea of **knowing** what life is and what it's supposed to be. This is so unbelievably wrong. Knowing is the opposite of living. If wondering is the beginning of life, curiosity is the next step, and knowing is the end.

The worst people on Earth are the people who think they know it all. They believe they have such an understanding of the Universe that they see what's best for them, *and best for you.* But imagine if those people who thought they knew everything took all that smug energy and used it to actually learn, understand, and become aware of the world around them.

You can do this. You can become the smartest person you've ever met by following one simple rule: admit to yourself that you don't know anything.

There are over seven billion people on this Earth. There are almost two hundred countries. There are over six thousand languages. One point two billion people speak Mandarin Chinese. You don't even speak the most common language on Earth. (Unless this is translated into Mandarin, in which case, "Nǐ hǎo, hěn gāoxìng rènshi nǐ!")

There will never be a time when you don't have more to learn. There will never be a moment when you even understand the moment you're in. You don't really understand the gravity that keeps your feet on the ground. You don't get how light passes through your eyes or how your brain translates those images. You don't comprehend how your ears process sounds. You don't even know the basics.

You're so arrogant. You just walk around in this miraculous body all over this miraculous planet and not a single second goes by when you actually know what's going on in a ten-foot radius around you, but somehow you're convinced you understand life and its workings?

The key to getting bigger and growing up is to admit you are small. The less you know, the more you can wonder, and the more you can stop being a narcissistic shithead and start living an interesting life.

And living an interesting life is all about one thing: curiosity.

Curiosity killed the cat because the cat wasn't hiding in its studio apartment eating freezer-burned Ben and Jerry's and being terrified of the world. That cat died doing what it loved: being a fucking cat.

Without curiosity, life is flat and beige and terrible. Don't you want to know what everything feels like? Don't you want to travel to the other side of the world? Don't you want to try to figure out why you're here?

Curiosity is the thing that gets you on a plane and occasionally makes you jump out of one (preferably with a parachute attached, unless you run Breitbart). Curiosity lets you discover new foods and cities and sex positions. All our heroes were curious. Inventors, explorers, and pioneers didn't stand on mountaintops screaming "I know!" Instead, they all asked the same question: "What if?"

It may seem like I've wandered off track and, god forbid, started to sound (shudder) motivational. But this is all to say that you really need to dismiss all the ideas of greatness you have been convinced to have about yourself.

"But what about confidence?" you ask, stupidly.

There is significantly more confidence in admitting that you don't know than in proclaiming that you do. Going into a future you're confident about isn't brave. It's easy. Walking blindly into the wilderness, knowing not what lies ahead? That's bravery. That's living. That's how you become an astronaut. The first people on the moon didn't really know what it was going to be like. They went there hoping to find out.

Thinking you're smart. Thinking you're great. These things feel good, but they're **never** useful. There is more to explore. There is more to find out there.

As a reminder: you're not that great. And in any moments when you feel like you might actually be great, you need to fight that urge with all of your might. The only way to attain greatness is to constantly and eternally reject it.

chapter seven

how to regret every moment of your life up until now

The greatest motivator of all is discontent!

—Jenny Mollen (author)

By now, we've established that positivity and the unquenchable thirst for happiness are invisible forces of destruction in your life. You're already a more complete and capable person for having taken steps to eliminate them.

But there are other emotions, ones you've spent your whole life trying to suppress, that are actually trying to help you. Deep inside you there is a feeling that just wants to shake things up and change the way you look at the world. If your life is stagnant and you're not getting the things you want, do not fear. There is a stick of TNT in your gut that's just aching to have its wick lit and knock some motherfucking sense into you:

That emotion is regret.

Yes, regret, the thing that everyone tells you not to have, is perhaps the most vital tool in your body. You've been told that regret is a waste of time, so you've never really addressed it properly. But don't pretend regret hasn't found a way to make itself a huge part of your life anyway.

Those nights that you lie awake and think about all the things you've ever done wrong. That feeling in the pit of your stomach when you say something that crosses the line when you're fighting with a relative or friend. That sinking feeling when you get back in your car after a date when you wanted to kiss him or her and you didn't because you were scared and now they think you're not into them and it's a total turnoff and you're probably going to be alone forever so you might as well buy some porn and pick up an inflatable sex doll at the store.

Regret is powerful. It stays in your body. Like swallowed gum, regret just lives in your intestines and bowels until the day you die. When they dump your body into the ground, over half of your body weight is just untapped regret. What if instead of letting it weigh you down, you could make regret one of the most important building blocks of your psyche?

You can. But people are hesitant to do so because regret is often coupled with shame. Regret requires admitting that you've done something wrong. People HATE that. People hate admitting they've made a mistake, because in this life, you don't get any do-overs. Sure, you can take an action to try to make the next thing better. But you can't undo what you've done. People can't deal with the shame of making mistakes or of having been wrong, so they convince themselves that they have no regrets as a form of self-protection.

They say that they don't have regrets because "they've learned from all the things that have happened in their lives and those experiences are exactly what have made them the person they are today."

If you hear someone talk like this, run for the fucking hills. You are within the grasp of a narcissistic, delusional lunatic.

Let's break it down for a moment, shall we?

IF a person has no regrets

BECAUSE the things they have learned from the things they've done wrong

HAVE made them into the person they are today

THEN that must mean they have no problems with the person they are today,

WHICH MEANS they must think they're pretty fucking exceptional.

RUN. FOR. THE. HILLS.

I can't imagine the same person would have the audacity to walk up to you and look you in the eye and tell you that they think they are perfect. I can't imagine they have the chutzpah to tell you that there's not one way in which they could be improved. Yet, for some reason, because they have used convoluted logic and detached themselves entirely from the very words that they're spouting, they're willing to tell you that they're perfect simply by saying something else: "I have no regrets!"

Are you really so pompous as to think the "person you are today" is somehow necessarily a good thing? Even if you do consider yourself a wonderful person, aren't there always ways you could be better? Could you have been smarter or kinder or more giving or more loving? If nothing else, could the "person you are today," at the very least, have been intelligent enough to know that eschewing regrets for the sake of feeling like your current state is something that others should be in awe of is a gross miscalculation and a super sad and masturbatory way to live your life? Maybe. In fact, definitely.

You should have a million regrets. The first one should be ever uttering the phrase "I have no regrets," and you should pinch yourself extra hard right in the nipple every time you say it from now on because that's probably the only way you're ever going to grow out of it. Regrets are EXACTLY the kinds of tools a person needs in order to have any chance of self-improvement.

Think about the worst thing you've ever done. Really think about it. Think about the people involved and about all the ripple effects. Think about the times you thought back to it or felt bad and it kept you up at night. Think about all the times you didn't have the courage to admit you were wrong or the apology that eventually came but took too long. Think about all the time and mental dexterity that went into finding ways to blame others and make whatever thing it was not your fault.

You're going to erase all that work from your mind? You're going to not utilize that to improve? No, you just need to feel good about yourself. Is that it?

When you're a kid and you put your hand on a hot stove and

it burns you, you learn not to do that again, right? This is one of those monstrously shitty examples that people use to teach dumb kids dumb things: a learning experience. I never put my hand on a hot stove. I've made so many mistakes in my life I can barely count them, but I never put my hand on a hot stove, and that's because I listened to people who told me not to put my hand on a hot stove.

"But I did put my hand on a hot stove and all my fingers look like overcooked bacon but I have no regrets because it made me the person I am today!"

And what are you? A person who put his hand on a hot stove and never will again. Well, I didn't even have to learn that lesson. And my fingers look pretty normal. Don't you see the problem here? You didn't need to be the asshole who put his hand on a hot stove in order to learn not to do that. You just needed to shut the fuck up for a second and pay attention to the experiences of people around you. You know what made me better? NOT putting my hand on a hot stove. I knew that if I could listen to the things people were telling me and then take the time to judge their veracity, I would probably be able to not burn my hand to the point where I couldn't masturbate for weeks. Although, if living regret-free still appeals to you, maybe you're better off having put your hand on a hot stove. In fact, maybe you should do it again. Over and over. You can just keep learning more and more! How exciting for you! No regrets!

There are currently billions of people on this Earth who have gone through stuff. There are millions of books (including this one) that are just chock-full of information. You DON'T need to learn all the lessons that life has in store for you yourself. Here are some examples:

You don't need to get syphilis to know that you probably don't want to have syphilis.

You don't need to get punched in the face by Ronda Rousey to know it would probably hurt.

You don't need to sit through a seminar by a self-help expert to know that they're going to take your two hundred bucks and buy another gold bidet to wash their butthole with while you walk away with nothing more than a very temporary sense of self-satisfaction that will evaporate as soon as you walk into a bar and realize that no one wants to talk to you and you take four shots of whiskey to ease the pain and then stumble by the 7-Eleven to pick up a mini pepperoni pizza to sadly microwave alone in your apartment while you cry all over your wood laminate floors and send texts to your ex that say things like, "Do you ever think about me?" at three o'clock in the morning every single day for four months straight while staring at their Facebook profile where they're obviously in a very happy relationship with that guy Roger whom you hate until they eventually block your number and you're just pissing into the wind (not that I have any experience with that EXACT thing many times in my life and am afraid to even mention it because Roger is probably going to write a letter to the publisher of this book telling me not to use the name Roger in this book but honestly I DON'T GIVE A FUCK, FUCK YOU, ROGER, YOU'RE A PIECE OF SHIT!).

You don't need to do that.

I've already done it for you.

Sure, you've heard it a million times. What doesn't kill you makes you stronger, right? Well, not really.

What doesn't kill you is all part of the series of events that will eventually kill you.

Every cigarette you smoke doesn't kill you, but it doesn't make you stronger either. In fact, all the little mistakes you make are like cigarettes. They may not be doing the final deed and you may not even feel them at all, but slowly, slowly, they are accumulating in your body, slowly making you worse and quietly shortening and worsening your life, until the mutations are out of control and then you have lung cancer and then in three months you're dead. No regrets!

If the reason you have no regrets is because it's made you into the person you are today, at this point I must once again remind you that you're not that great. You're not perfect. You're not the end of a grand series of decisions the Universe has made in order to create the one perfect "you." If you can look in a mirror and say, "I would change nothing," then you should just keep standing in front of that mirror and keep saying that over and over again until the day you're dead, because I can guarantee you that no one on Earth wants to be around you.

Don't be afraid of your regrets.

Don't be afraid to say you're sorry.

Don't be afraid to say you're bad.

Don't be afraid to say you fucked everything up again.

This is the only way you're ever going to get any better. This is the only way a human being can go from "not great" to "maybe a little less not great."

Don't run from your regrets. USE THEM.

Instead of thinking of regrets as things that hold you back and make you sad, think of how your regrets can mold and define your movements. Think of your regrets as warnings. Think of your mistakes as land mines, but now that you've stepped on them, you know exactly where they are...

You wouldn't walk through a battle zone blindfolded if you had the option of looking at a map, so why would you go through life with your eyes covered by a thick layer of gross and unnecessary self-love?

Regrets are markers on the map of your life. It can be fun if you think of it like a treasure map in your mind, but instead of finding gold at the end, your reward is just not royally fucking up your life.

But then things start getting a little more complicated. First and foremost, your goals will begin to shift and become more refined. When you're eighteen, your goals are usually limited to:

1. Have enough money to Netflix and Chill.
2. Find someone who wants to touch your genitals with their mouth.
3. Get alcohol illegally.

When you turn twenty-one, things change dramatically:

1. Have enough money to Netflix and Chill.
2. Find someone who wants to touch your genitals with their mouth.
3. Get alcohol legally.

But then you start to get a little bit older and you start to have real goals. Let's look at one of these possible goals. Let's imagine that your goal is to start a family, and in order to do that, you need to find the right life partner, someone you can love and respect and grow with and learn from and take criticism from AND also think they're cute enough to want them to be the only one to touch your genitals with their mouth for as long as you live. This is exactly where your regrets will begin to come in handy.

Now I want you to think about all the relationships you've ever had and instead of thinking about "how much you grew" or "how young you were," just be super honest with yourself and write down THE THINGS YOU REGRET.

Did you cheat on them? Did they cheat on you and you let them get away with it? Were you too controlling? Were you mean? Ask yourself these questions and instead of thinking about how much they suck (and I'm sure they do; exes are garbage and should all be forced to go live on a remote island together where they are required to make each other unhappy and fake orgasms for all eternity like they're in some kind of shitty relationship purgatory), think about how much YOU suck, just for a minute.

I can guarantee that you weren't perfect. I guarantee that you did things wrong. Sometimes the wrong things you do are actually really simple. Did you stay with them after you knew it should have been over? Did you pretend they were great because you knew your family hated them and you subconsciously wanted to prove them wrong? Did you use them to get back at another piece-of-shit ex? Or were you just not honest with yourself about what you wanted?

If you've been honest with yourself up to this point, you can take this information and finally step out into the terrifying mine-field that is dating. If you try hard enough, you may actually refrain from making the same exact mistakes you've made before. Go ahead and take a look at your mental map now. You can see which paths lead forward and which paths lead to a dead end.

You'll see that the road between you and your goals is much clearer. All the problems along the way are all right there in front of you and you now have the information you need to not make the same mistakes again. The odds of you failing are lower.

But this can only happen if you ignore the voice that lives inside of you and tells you that you're great. You MUST see your faults as faults in order to improve them. If I were to call up every one of your exes and ask them to tell me all the things that are wrong with you, there's a really good chance they would all say the same thing. Because instead of actually changing, you're only changing YOUR perspective.

(And if you think this doesn't apply directly to sex too, you are absolutely wrong. There is a pretty damn good chance you've never given anyone an orgasm that made them shake like a tased horse, and that's because whenever things haven't gone well in the bedroom, you've blamed things like chemistry, whiskey dick, or cotton crotch, and you never had the courage to go back and ask the person what you were doing wrong down there. This is a good time to take a second, put down the book, call an ex, and ask them what the worst part of being with you, sexually, was. It's a super uncomfy call, but if you have the guts to make it, you may actually *improve* your performance. Life isn't all about sex. But it doesn't hurt. Unless you're doing it wrong. Well, sometimes. Okay, moving on . . .)

You see, your regrets aren't holding you back. Pretending you don't have any is. And you've always subconsciously known this, even back when you were a kid.

Do you remember Mario? You know, he's the plumber with the asexual brother and some regal girlfriend who's either always getting kidnapped or maybe she just likes taking vacations with other men in giant castles all over the world. I've had a girlfriend or two who had that proclivity also.

Well, when you played *Super Mario Brothers 1, 2, 3, World,* or whatever, you were actually accidentally learning some pretty great tools for getting through life. And it's not just that if you eat mushrooms and put on a raccoon suit, things get a lot more fun.

Everything you ever needed to learn about regrets and about taking risks to get rewards was neatly packaged for you in that little game.

At the beginning of every level you knew exactly where you were. You could run as much as you wanted to the left of the screen but that was where the world ended. Just like in life, you can't go back in time and undo the things you've done. You're always at the beginning and the only way to go is forward.

Now, in *Super Mario Brothers* you have a goal and it's pretty clear what it is. You want to get the princess from the castle and you want to defeat the bad guy on your way there. But you don't really know the big picture exactly. I mean, every time you get to the end, the princess is already in another castle and there's just some weird mushroom-headed dude there yelling and jumping around being unhelpful (and you're thinking, "Why don't you ever stop her from leaving? What the fuck is wrong with you? You're just hanging around here screaming and hopping and making me crazy."). So you don't really know where life is going to take you and you don't really know if you're ever going to reach "the end" but you know that you're not going to get any closer unless you actually just push that little button and move across the screen to the right.

At first, you're constantly dying. You get tripped up by an errant turtle shell or eaten by some kind of toothy flower or shot by one of those sideways bullets that's always flying around and making you wonder why the residents of Mario World have never passed any kind of meaningful gun control laws. It can be really frustrating. You just die over and over again and that sad music plays, mocking you.

But then you start to realize something. Almost all of these stray bullets and these vicious turtles and these ravenous blood-sucking flowers...they're kind of predictable. They all more or less move in the same ways and when you focus on what they do and what you know about them, well, it becomes significantly easier to avoid them entirely (or to violently murder one of said turtles and use his corpse as a weapon against one of his relatives).

And every time you do something wrong and forget what you know, or every time you encounter a new enemy you aren't familiar with, and you die, you have two choices: You can say, "I played with no regrets," and continue haphazardly, making it no closer to the goal than before, or you can say, "Here's what I did wrong," and correct your course. You can change your methods and your ways, change your speed and direction. You can change everything, and you will, if and only if you allow yourself to feel the emotional loss of Mario falling thousands of feet from the clouds into the murky abyss.

Now, you can totally play that first way, have no regrets, and have a lot of fun. But if you're that kind of player, you don't know that there are many other worlds out there, and so many fun levels in each world. You're also not getting any better. You wouldn't survive in those worlds anyway.

But if you play the second way, maybe you'll have a little less fun in the short term. You'll be thinking critically and perhaps enjoying the process a little less. But the overall experience will be so much more full and so much more diverse that in the end you'll have used your lives more effectively. You have to experience the regrets fully and deeply in order to gain the requisite expertise to rise to the challenge of the next level.

And that, my friends, is how you eventually end up with the princess. (Bonus: you also get a castle and you finally get that damned mushroom-headed idiot to stop yelling at you.)

And if you don't learn from your regrets, you end up spending the rest of your life in a shitty castle in the middle of nowhere with Toad.

So I guess in some ways Mario is a lot like dating.

But taking your regrets and making a mental map doesn't

just apply to love and genital licking. It applies to literally EVERYTHING.

Once again, it's clear to see that the things that you think have been conspiring to work against you can actually be made to work FOR YOU.

Have regrets!

Learn from them!

Make fewer mistakes!

Become better!

This is how you become less not great.

frustration!

If you've ever seen Iliza Shlesinger perform live, then you've watched stand-up comedy at its best. She's a brilliant rapid-fire monologist, an effusive ball of energy, and simply one of the funniest people you can meet. But at the heart of what will become our entertainment, there is a core of frustration that comes from a whole life of feeling left out.

Of course we have all felt left out from time to time, but Iliza grew up as a Jew in Texas with an unspellable last name who wasn't "pretty enough to be the pretty one, but not dorky or quirky or weird enough either," she says. Through this, and maybe because of this, she became an incredibly successful comic in a male-dominated landscape.

"When I was young I always felt like my mom had to remind people that I was there. I have vivid memories of her going into random administration offices for school or temple and having to clear up some mix-up with my name. I also moved schools a lot. I never really had a core group of girlfriends, and you know it's already hard to make friends with little girls. I always felt like I was on the outside. I didn't even get into the colleges I thought I should get into, never made varsity right away—I just never clicked with a group.

"And then I moved to LA and I wasn't really part of anything. I wasn't a 'New York comic' or a 'Chicago comic.' I wasn't part of an alt-comic group. I was never in a writers' room with a bunch of people working together to make comedy. I was alone. Stand-up is such a solo gig."

But I love Iliza because like all good artists, she took that feeling and struck at the core of what frustrates all of us about the world. "I get angry very quickly. I'm constantly frustrated. In my act I definitely talk about the things that frustrate me with society, with how women are treated, how we perceive other humans, how I feel as an American. Compound that with how things move so slowly in Hollywood, it could be easy to become perma-frustrated." She stopped waiting for opportunities and started creating them. Now, with three Netflix specials under her belt, her own TV show, and her book *Girl Logic: The Genius and the Absurdity*, Iliza doesn't feel as left out anymore.

"I felt left out my whole life so I created a job where I can include everyone. My audience and my fans make me feel so loved. I am frustrated with people so I created a job where I can call people out. I was frustrated with Hollywood so I created my own career where I can make my own opportunities."

Iliza knows that frustration is part of what makes her so relatable as a performer. "If I wasn't frustrated, I would be another average white comic."

chapter eight

don't pretend to be
better than you are.
pretend to be worse.

The biggest mistake people make when trying to reach their goals is pretending to be better than they are. Fake it 'til you make it! Act as if! Dress for the job you want, not the job you have!

Terrible advice.

The problem is that most people aren't that dumb. They're not as easily fooled as you think, especially when everyone is trying to fool them the same way. Acting like you know everything is such an incredible turnoff, and worse than that, it's totally transparent. People succeed and get better by admitting what they do not know, not by highlighting what they do know. I'm going to use job interviews and getting a job as an example here, but try to understand that this kind of thought process applies to everything. Everything in life is kind of like a job interview. Don't fuck it up.

Ask yourself this question: if you were hiring a pilot to fly a plane with you and your family on it, would you rather put your life in the hands of a person who asks a few questions and makes sure that everything is in order, or a person who looks at the plane and says, "Yeah, looks fine, no problem, I can fly anything!"?

As someone who has conducted a lot of job interviews, I can tell you that one of the most informative questions that you can ask is: "What is your worst quality?"

We've all seen the after-school specials and the shitty instructional videos that teach you how to answer this question. They tell you to take all of your best attributes (or at least the ones you think are going to impress your potential employer) and make them sound like they're bad. You know, the usual:

"I care too much. I bring my work home with me, and I don't shut off my brain!"

"I make myself too available. My phone is never off and I am always ready to work! Literally any hour of the day! I have to work on that!"

"I'm unbelievably hardworking and endlessly committed to the job and I will literally do anything you need at all hours. I don't even need food or water. I am a working robot that will make all your wildest dreams come true. Obviously, I need to work on that!"

When someone said something like that to me, a smile emerged on my face. I knew that I would literally never see that person again as long as I lived. Beyond the obvious issue, which is that they are so spectacularly transparent in their lies (if you're going to lie, lie better), the real issue is that this person clearly hasn't learned anything from any of the places they've worked before.

You can't hide your worst qualities. They will always come out. They will betray you. You can only pretend to be great for so long before you'll be discovered. And when you're discovered with all those bad qualities, not only are you a person with those bad qualities; you're also a person who lied about having them (or even worse, doesn't know WHAT their bad qualities are).

Are you hardheaded and stubborn? Are you always late? Do you fight easily with coworkers? Are you hypercompetitive? Do you get mad when you don't get your way? Do you hate being wrong? Do you want to murder all your coworkers when they bring salmon in for lunch and put it in the microwave and it cooks for too long and then the salmon juice starts popping all over the glass and then they just leave it there like nothing happened and then for the rest of the year everything you put in the microwave has a fishy after-taste, what were you raised in a fucking barn, Brenda?

So right now you're probably thinking, "Sure, a lot of those things are me, but there is NO WAY in hell I would ever admit to that in a job interview." Well, this is precisely where you're wrong. The world is competitive, jobs are hard to get and keep, and if you keep repeating all the lies you and EVERYONE ELSE are always telling, you'll keep having the same results you've always had.

Let's take a look at some of those negative attributes and see if there's actually more to them than meets the eye. And for the record, every single negative attribute listed above describes me, and they have all been instrumental in my professional growth over the last fifteen years.

I am hardheaded and stubborn. I hate being wrong. I am so passionate about being right that even when I start to get the inkling that I might be wrong about something (which is obviously almost never), I would rather bend reality and change everything in the world to fit my point of view than change my point of view to reflect the world. And in one of those very, very, very rare instances where I may possibly be wrong, well, I will change my point of view and then virulently defend my previous position as the most correct position at the time prior to the changing of my mind. Sounds like a pretty contentious and difficult way to live, right? Can you imagine dating me? It's a fucking nightmare. But you're not interviewing me to see if you want to date me. You're interviewing me to see if you want me on your team, and if I'm interviewing someone to be on my team, I want a person who doesn't ever take their foot off the gas pedal. I don't want to be your friend, but, boy, do I want to be on your side. Sometimes, the best person you can have in your life is a person you'd absolutely hate to have as your enemy because they're so insistent and powerful that the world gives in to their will.

I hate not getting my way. I hate it more than anything. And when it happens, I make sure to not let it happen again, and if it happens again, I make DAMN SURE to not let it happen after that. I pout, I mope, I cry, and I give a shit to the point where I can barely function anymore, and all I'm able to do is sit at home and watch cartoons from my childhood on YouTube in a feeble attempt to awaken the soul of the child who's buried deep within me who hasn't given up on life yet.

I also get unbelievably angry with people I work with who don't agree with me. And I expect them to get as angry with me as I am with them. Isn't that why we all do things? Don't we all want to do the best possible version of whatever we do? When I worked in a video store (for you young people out there, a video store is like, instead of your home screen on Netflix, people used to go to a big building, and inside that building you could find all the movies in these little boxes and you would walk up and just pick the movie you wanted, just like pointing a mouse but instead of a mouse it was just your hand and instead of clicking you just picked it up and took it home and then you would bring it back the next day. Weird, I know, honestly, it makes so little sense now that it's actually kind of hard to explain), I came into work every single day and put on my shitty white-ruffled tuxedo shirt and my clip-on red bow tie and my popcorn-print vest and I tried to be the best and the fastest and the most passionate. I alphabetized the shit out of those movies. I made sure people paid their late fees. I could rewind three movies at a time with my eyes closed. And it's not because I love corporate America or because I ever thought I had a huge future in video-store management (and thank god for that because I would've gotten a very rude awakening eventually) but because I looked around me and saw a competition that I wanted to win. And the desire to win is born in the inherent knowledge that you are a loser. If you're a winner and you think you are, why bother trying hard? But if you're a loser and you hate it, man, you'll do whatever you can in the world to make sure that you win.

But yeah, tell me more about how you care too much. You're not even good at lying. You think I'm going to hire you? And fuck you and fuck your salmon, Brenda...

So what am I saying with all of this?

I guess more than anything I'm trying to show that people are willing to spend a tremendous amount of time and energy to try to feel good about the position they're in and will usually put almost no energy at all into changing their position so that it actually IS GOOD. You're so busy working on your fake smile you forget to actually do the things that might one day make you smile authentically.

After all, they say it takes seventeen muscles to smile and forty-three muscles to frown (by the way, this is wrong, but if it were right) and when going through life, you're better off using the muscles you have instead of letting them lie dormant, atrophying and eventually looking like your face is melting off and needs Botox.

So, turn that smile upside down.

vengeance!

Travon Free was born in Compton, California. "Statistically, I should be dead," he says. But he's not dead. This thirty-two-year-old man is an Emmy-winning television writer with a million projects on the horizon. Things weren't always easy, though.

In 2012, Travon took his last shot at success when he submitted a packet to become a writer for *The Daily Show with Jon Stewart*. The producers of the show called him to tell him that while he was very good, there simply wasn't a place on the staff for him. He met with them the day before the Emmy Awards in 2012. "It was fucking awful. I remember sitting on the couch and my sister and uncle were at my apartment. I felt so fucking crushed. I'm sitting there and trying so hard not to cry. I don't know what to do."

Travon didn't feel hope in this moment. He didn't feel confident everything was going to work out. "I was literally digging through my couch to find change to buy food. I wasn't even embarrassed. I would go to the drive-through and just pay people with change. Give me whatever off the dollar menu."

Travon gave up. "I applied for a park ranger job. A city job with benefits. But they didn't think I was qualified enough, even with my college degree." His life and his dreams were in the shitter. So what gave Travon the energy to keep pushing?

"I used a lot of vengeance as fuel. I wanted to succeed to really rub it in people's faces. In college I went through a bad breakup and I remember thinking to myself, I'm going to make it so this person has to see my face everywhere.

"I think the people who told me I couldn't do it were important. I don't know how hard I would have tried if people told me I could do it. We hate that people tell us that shit, but the opposite might be worse. We might not have seen the greatest people in the world do the things they did if they didn't have the negative fuel to drive them forward. If you're a parent and you want your kid to be great, just tell them they can't do anything. Even if you believe in them, tell them they'll never get their dreams. When people tell you that you can do and be anything, that makes it easier to give up on shit. Because you can always do something else."

When Travon got the call that another writer had been let go from *The Daily Show* and they were ready to hire him, he had four dollars in his bank account. He still has the bank statement as a reminder. In 2015, three years and a day after he was told his dreams were over, Travon won his first Emmy. He remembers one man in particular who told him he would never amount to anything: "No one knows who the fuck that guy is. I have two Emmys."

chapter nine

building a life that is less disappointing than the one you already have

I wake up every single day confident in the knowledge that I will never write another good song. I tend to internalize a lot of things I'm upset about and put them into songs. That's how I get it out of my head. When I was growing up, if I was mad or sad I would listen to music. So now, when I get mad, I try to use it in my music.

—Mark Hoppus (singer-songwriter, Blink-182)

At this point, I'm just going to assume that you're not afraid anymore. If you've gotten this far, it's because you see the value in coming to terms with the fact that you're not that great. But philosophy can only take you so far. What you need now is a plan of action. You need actual ways to start accomplishing all the shit you want to accomplish.

And this is where all the other self-help books have failed you. And everyone else. All the other self-help books basically tell you to do the same thing. They tell you that you're great and that you're important, and then they just leave you hanging out to dry, like a sex-soiled rag on the edge of the tub, telling you that you can just go about your life as you were before, but now with your new mentality, everything is suddenly going to go swimmingly. If you notice, this advice has done very little for anyone other than the authors, who have become fucking billionaires while you all just smile and laugh and smile and shit money into their bank accounts.

Okay, but enough about them. Let's talk about you. Let's talk about how we're going to make you less not great.

The key to building your new less not-great life is in taking the inevitable bad parts of life and, instead of avoiding them, making them work for you. Negative energy is incredibly powerful. It can take weeks to get in a good mood, but it only takes fifteen seconds for your neighbor Gary to open his shithole mouth and tell you something that completely ruins your day. It can take months to lose those last few pounds, but only a few minutes to eat two pepperoni pizzas and an entire sleeve of Thin Mints. It takes years to build a building, but it can be destroyed in just a few seconds. There's no question that negative energy is FUCKING POWERFUL. What if you could make that energy work FOR you instead of AGAINST you?

When people talk about things that they fear in life, most of them relate back to one thing: failure.

Failure is powerful because it really hits every emotional button. The fear of it stops you from trying to get the things you want. And when you finally work up the courage to try to overcome it, failure is the thing that robs you of whatever you wanted to begin with.

but how can you make failure your bitch?

People love talking about how many times successful people have failed. They love bringing up Michael Jordan being dropped from his high school basketball team. They love talking about everyone telling Thomas Edison he would never amount to anything. There is nothing more exciting than a comeback story: the story of someone who failed over and over and over and over again but those failures only made her or him stronger and then one day they broke through and became someone aspirational and inspirational. People use these examples as a way to tell you that failures are just stumbling blocks along the way. Not only do they want you to think of failures as part of your journey; they want you to think that success isn't possible without failures.

Sure, that may be true, but it totally negates the PURPOSE of failure and the FEELINGS that are supposed to accompany failure. When you fail, you're supposed to feel really fucking bad about yourself. You should feel like a stupid loser who is never going to amount to anything. When you fail, it's because you're not that great, and that's something that you need to KNOW and need to FEEL. When Michael Jordan got cut from his basketball team, he probably didn't jump up and down gleefully. "It was embarrassing not making the team," he said. He went home, locked himself in his room, and cried. Michael Jordan wasn't an incredible basketball player at that time, obviously. He wasn't even good enough to make his team, and as a result he felt like garbage. It was that exact feeling, that FEELING of failure and KNOWING that he wasn't good enough, that must have been one of the biggest parts of what gave him the inspiration to actually become good enough to eventually become Michael Jordan. "Whenever I was working out and got tired and figured I ought to stop, I'd close my eyes and see that list in the locker room without my name on it," Jordan explained in the *Newsweek Special Edition: Jordan: 30 Years Since MJ Changed the Game*. Instead of feeling good about himself, Jordan felt embarrassed and ashamed, and he USED those FEELINGS to push himself further.

There was another basketball player who got cut from his basketball team and got told, "Don't worry. This is all part of the process of becoming successful. This is what happened to Michael Jordan. So one day you're going to be a huge superstar." And do you know who that man was?

No, of course you fucking don't. Just like my DJ friend from Vermont.

You don't know him because he never made it to the NBA. He never made it back on any team ever, because instead of feeling like a piece of shit and knowing that he simply wasn't good enough, he was comforted with nonsense stories about how failure is part of the journey. And so he kept practicing exactly as hard as he always did (when in reality he should have been trying ten times harder) and that simply wasn't good enough. And now he probably tells people that he was going to be the next Michael Jordan, but it didn't happen, and that was all part of "the plan." (Because, you know, everything happens for a reason...)

Failure is an unbelievable driving force. It's negative and it's sad and it sucks and that is EXACTLY what makes it so powerful. People don't want to feel those things, so instead they placate themselves by telling themselves that failures are just hurdles in the race. But even people who run hurdles professionally don't think of hurdles as good things. They're actually very bad. They're in the fucking way.

Things in this world, especially emotions, aren't static. They're not the same all the time. As your life changes, as your situation changes, you can process and use your emotions differently. Sure, when you look back on the failures in your life, they had the potential to propel you forward, but it's NOT because they didn't feel like failures. When you fail you need to double down, work harder, be sadder than ever, and then find a way to crawl out of the dark hole of pizza boxes, Chinese takeout containers, and wine bottles, and get back into the light.

But first, you need to make failure your bitch. And the only way to do that is to **LET THE FAILURE WIN**. It's true. You need to let failure grab you by the balls or by the tits or by the taint and swing you around its head like an angry ogre. You need to be destroyed. You need to be that character in the horror film who's been stabbed in each leg, has a bullet in each hand, and has lost six pints of blood before you can miraculously kill the man in the mask and save the day. And that's the trick. It truly is.

You can't ever really beat failure. You will likely fail at almost everything you try. All your relationships will fail, except for one (hopefully). But while everyone else is out there fighting failure, you're just going to let failure win. Failure is like a bear. Just fall to the ground and let it maul you like Leonardo DiCaprio and then let it move on to something else. This is when you rise. This is when you can finally succeed. After failure has completed its task.

Failure, however, does not come alone. Before the big bear that is failure leaves the scene of the crime it takes a moment and squats down and takes three big old shits right there in the middle of the woods. And those shits are named shame, anxiety, and desperation. Or S.A.D.

S.A.D. are for many people the most powerful negative driving forces in their lives. But once you learn how to let failure do its work, you can now rock the living shit out of S.A.D.

shame—your new best friend

I'm not sure there is a more devastating feeling than shame. It can ruin lives. When you are truly and really ashamed, you feel subhuman. Often this lack of humanity makes it even worse. As a subhuman, you stop holding yourself to the same standards you would if you still considered yourself human.

This is where you find yourself having a little too much tequila with your cereal in the morning and vomiting in a fountain at the Mall of America just because you think things can't get any worse than they are. This is where you tell people you love that you don't love them, because you need to protect them from the horrible sewer creature that you've become. Shame takes the worst moments of your life and plays them back in your mind over and over and over and over again until the worst moments become part of every moment, even the best moments, and they color your every thought.

But as always, really powerful emotions don't have to just stick a pole up your ass and spin you around on it like a pig on a spit with an apple in its mouth. Shame may be the most devastating feeling of them all, but that also makes it the most powerful weapon for you to use against yourself. Earlier in the book we talked about how powerful an enemy can be. We all know that nuclear weapons are terrible and should never be used, but their mere existence works as a really great deterrent (and hopefully by the time you read this book we haven't gotten into a nuclear war and aren't all dead!). Shame is the nuclear bomb in the emotion arsenal. You can either let the world use it on you or you can threaten to use it on yourself.

I'll tell you how I did exactly that.

I hate everything about my parents' genes. I am crooked-toothed and short and have unwieldy hair. But there is nothing I hate more than how fat my body always wants to be.

I was a fat little kid, and other than a brief flirtation with anorexia, I was always fat. I hid it well with baggy clothes and by having big hair and a big beard to cover up my lumpy hot-dog-package neck. But no matter what I wore, my thighs always scraped together and gave me rashes when I would run (which was almost never). I was fat to a point where I couldn't even find a place to put my testicles when I lay on my side. I couldn't stuff them between my thighs because they would get smushed. I couldn't just push them out in front of me because, well, that's not where testicles are supposed to go. I slept on my back, but my neck fat crushed my esophagus and I would cough myself awake several times a night. And nobody ever really told me I was fat (except for one guy, FUCK YOU, CHRIS), and that made things worse. I was ashamed and no one would let me feel ashamed because they wanted me to be positive and happy. They meant well, but they also always handed me an extra-large serving of cake at their birthday parties.

Now, before we get into a whole argument, there is absolutely nothing wrong with being fat. Or skinny. Or anything. Be whatever you want to be. I just personally didn't like my body. I wanted to look different than I did. I think it's wonderful that my friends didn't shame me. But I wish I had learned to shame myself earlier. For myself. For the things that I wanted. PLEASE don't think this is intended to tell you to change into what you think someone else wants you to be. If you're happy with your body, that is wonderful. I'm sure there are lots of other things about you that need improvement anyway. But this was how *I* felt, by *myself,* about *my body.* I hope you're happy with yours, but if you're not, and if there's something you can do about it, then this is a good way.

I pretend to be 5'8" because one time a doctor told me I was 5'8". It's not a lie. He just probably gave me an extra inch and I choose to believe his truth. But let's imagine I'm 5'7". On May 30, 2015, I got on a scale and I weighed 213.9 pounds. And it freaked me the fuck out. I told some friends and they all pretty much uniformly furrowed their brows but inevitably said some form of "you look pretty good, considering." They would not shame me. They are lovely and entirely too damn nice.

As you might be aware, for a long time I was a producer on several popular dating shows. I don't know if you've seen these shows, but one thing a majority of the participants have in common is that they're in really good physical shape. They're athletic and many of them are body builders or personal trainers or Pilates experts or raw-food enthusiasts. These are people who care about, and care for, their bodies. It's easy to discount people like that and assume that's all there is to them, but some of these people are my closest friends. They're interesting and complex and full of life and stories. They're just normal people like me and you except they look like someone carved them out of stone while I look like someone squeezed me out of a Play-Doh container.

We were just about to start shooting one of these shows in a beautiful, beachy location when I had my dreadful weigh-in. Here I was, my fattest ever (and not just fat, truly out of shape—I hadn't worked out in nearly a year), about to be surrounded for a summer by people with perfectly sculpted abs. But it was okay; I would just do what I always did. I would wear funky T-shirts that would distract everyone from my jiggling man-titties. And even though I knew no one cared what I looked like shirtless, I wasn't going to give anyone that mental image. I would've been so ashamed.

And that's when I had an idea: *What if I never wear a shirt?*

What if instead of hiding from the shame I feel, I force it, and my jiggling man-titties, into the light?

So that's what I did. For those terrifying few weeks I spent every single free moment on a beautiful beach with my shirt off. There it was, my bulbous gut in plain view at all times. It was a fact that anyone within a hundred-yard radius could see my pasty white shame. And I hated it. I hated every second of it. To be honest, I'm pretty sure no one even noticed or cared, but the way I *felt*, well, that was quickly becoming too painful to bear. By the second week I knew I had to do something. I started jogging on the beach. If you think walking around in that environment with your shirt off is embarrassing, try jogging on the beach when you can barely jog for a minute straight without running out of breath. The muscular men on the beach would literally walk beside me, keeping up with my shameful jogging pace. They would never say anything. They were kind. But I could feel my own self-hatred turning into something else: determination.

By the end of the month, I was running a mile, which is something I didn't think I'd ever be able to do. And even after the show was over, I went home and every morning I stood in front of the mirror and I stared at the body I hated. I took my shirt off when I went to the beach. I wore tank tops to the gym. I exposed my body and my shame.

Soon I was running three miles a day, five days a week. One time I ran eight and a half miles. One time I ran ten. I couldn't believe it. I got workout DVDs and wheezed along to them every single day. Every day I felt the eyes of my friends and my coworkers on me. I KNEW they weren't judging me. I knew they loved me for who I was. The shame was coming from inside the house. I hated my body for me. With every run, with every meal, with every skipped dessert, I thought of how I chose to see myself through the nonexistent judgmental eyes of others. I SHAMED THE LIVING FUCK OUT OF MYSELF.

And soon enough I was 175 pounds. I even hit 171 pounds for a little while. I had lost 42 pounds in about five months. And I've kept it off. And to this day I wake up every morning and I don't think about what I feel good about when it comes to my body. I think about those first few days of shirtlessness on the beach. I don't ever want to feel that way about myself again.

I shoved shame up my ass and shit out over 40 pounds. I didn't let the world shame me. I beat myself to it. That's how I used shame to change.

anxiety—the world's biggest asshole

Anxiety is that little voice in your head that tells you everything is about to go wrong. It's like an unbelievably shitty and loud alarm clock that you just can't seem to get rid of. For the few weeks that you own it, the clock just goes off at random hours of the night. It's loud and terrible like a fire alarm and it scares you. Sometimes it goes off just a few minutes after you hit snooze the first time. Sometimes it doesn't go off at all, and you oversleep and you miss your flight and your whole family is mad at you because you ruined Christmas. Eventually, it doesn't even matter if it goes off anymore. You can't sleep. You can't relax. You can't ever have a moment of peace because you're always just on the edge of terror. To be clear, anxiety is an asshole.

But maybe you don't need to relax. Maybe you don't need a moment of peace. Maybe you haven't earned it yet. People in your life (usually with very good intentions) will tell you to be easy on yourself. They'll tell you to have a little bit of dessert because you've had a rough day even when you're trying to diet and you know it's a bad idea. They'll tell you that you work too hard and you need to take a vacation even though you know what you really need is a raise and a promotion. People see tension and anxiety and angst in you and they want to calm it. That's NOT because anxiety is bad for you. It's because it's uncomfortable FOR THEM. Don't get me wrong. They don't want to hurt you. They just haven't accepted some basic truths about life. They haven't accepted that attaining success and accomplishing your goals is HARD AS FUCK and often VERY PAINFUL.

But you know better than that by now. You know that pain is PART OF IT.

I take vacations pretty regularly now. I find a weekend or two to go out of town when I can. Sometimes I leave for a whole week and (unsuccessfully try to) just forget about work and all my obligations. But to this day, I know I would be closer to my goals if I didn't do this. I'm willing to make those concessions now, but it took a long, long while to get there.

My annual salary the first year I decided I was only going to work in television was well under $10,000. Thankfully I had some help (I was living back at home), but it wasn't much. My second year I made $23,000. And I had a boss that year who gave me some really great advice. I had asked him how much I should try to work as a freelance TV producer, and how much time I should take off to try to have fun. He laughed and told me this: don't EVER take a vacation until you have $100,000. Then you can afford to take some risks. Holy shit, I thought, my head flooding with the fear of missing out. Think of all the trips I'll miss. All the weddings and funerals. All the good times my friends will have while I'm working. But he was right and I knew it. Let's just say I didn't take a vacation for a long, long time. I was stressed and I was sad and I was anxious and I cried ALL the time.

And now I take vacations. And they're even better because I remember how fucking terrible it felt to never take one.

Maybe you don't need that day off. Maybe you don't need to sleep in. Maybe you don't need to go hang out with your friends. Fuck it, maybe you do, DO WHATEVER YOU WANT, but FEEL THE ANXIETY. FEEL IT and use it. NEVER RELAX.

This isn't about what *I* think success is. This is about what YOU think success is. This isn't about money or status or fame or anything like that. It's about YOUR dreams. And I hope your dreams are big and bold and crazy and wild and goddamn nearly impossible to reach. Your dreams should fill you with dread and anxiety. You should live in perpetual uneasiness because you know you MAY NOT get to live your dreams. And then maybe you'll work hard enough to actually get there. Use that anxiety. Use that unpredictable alarm clock to keep you on your toes and stay vigilant and active until you have the motherfucking things you want.

desperation—all you need is nothing

We've all heard of rock bottom. All the greatest movies make use of rock bottom to propel the main character forward towards their eventual victory. Why can't you do the same? Peter Parker loses Mary Jane. Fredo betrays his brother. Rachel McAdams marries that other guy instead of Ryan Gosling. All the best stories use this clever device to show the trajectory of success. And it's not an accident. It's a real thing. There's nothing quite like having nothing to lose—or even better, having nothing—to force you to get the fuck out there and make something of your life.

If you've already hit rock bottom, then you know it doesn't last forever. If you haven't yet, you need to know that it won't. I think one of the most successful and magical people I know is James Gunn, who wrote and directed *Guardians of the Galaxy* and made almost a billion dollars with *Guardians of the Galaxy Vol. 2*. I asked him what the most important emotion for him was in his professional success. His answer came easily and quickly: "Desperation." It was knowing there were no other options for him that left success as his only way forward. And he felt that desperation so deeply, to his core, that he came out the other end of that desperation on top of the world. In fact, he even created new worlds and took his audiences to places that have never existed before. That's what a desperate imagination can do for you.

Now, look, you're not James Gunn and neither am I, but we can do things the exact same way. Desperation is beautiful because it's so limiting and restricting. Barry Schwartz, in his 2005 TED Talk "The Paradox of Choice," tells us about how too many options lead people to freeze up instead of making a choice at all. One hundred and seventy-five salad dressings are too many, he says. There's so much pressure to be right and to pick correctly that most people can't pick at all. Why is it so hard? Well, as the 2002 Steven Spielberg miniseries *Taken* reminds us, "Every choice is the death of all other possibilities." People are afraid to make choices because every step in one direction is a step away from all other directions. But you can't walk towards several places at once. There's no question that people don't often get to be what they want to be because they want to be too many things. They won't make a choice. They're *afraid* to make a choice.

But once they make one, they have a chance. You have to remember that it's almost impossible to succeed at ANYTHING, much less at SEVERAL THINGS AT ONCE. Honestly, who the fuck do you think you are? You're one of seven billion people competing for a tiny piece of the pie. At least decide what fucking flavor you want before you take a swing at the crust. If you spend your life trying to be the world's greatest actor / investment banker / inventor / food photographer / model / hedge fund manager / dictator of a small Polynesian island / dancer, chances are you're not going to become any of those things. At least not all at once.

THIS IS WHERE YOU MUST BEGIN TO SEE ROCK BOTTOM AS YOUR FRIEND, NOT YOUR ENEMY. HERE IS WHERE YOU MUST ABANDON HOPE. HOPE IS YOUR ENEMY. HOPE IS THE AUNT WHO TELLS YOU YOU'RE A GREAT SINGER AND THEN YOU END UP IN AN *AMERICAN IDOL* COMMERCIAL AND THAT'S ALL THAT HAPPENS TO YOU FOR THE REST OF YOUR LIFE.

But most readers of this book are actually quite lucky. Most of them have never really hit rock bottom. Most of them never feel real desperation. That's great, as far as your humanity goes. And if you have, then you know that you should be glad if other people haven't.

And that's why you have to begin to manufacture desperation in your mind. You must occasionally allow the voices in your head to tell you that you are never going to have the things you want. It's counterintuitive because you've trained yourself to quiet the voices when they tell you that your failure and death are imminent. Everyone does that. But not anymore. YOU ARE GOING

TO DO THE OPPOSITE. Every time a shred of doubt pops into your mind, you are going to close your eyes and try to listen to that evil little voice. Right now that voice is quiet and buried deep in the bowels of your soul. Or maybe just in your bowels. It's small and it's quiet and it can't hurt you. But now you're going to begin to raise it like a precious child. You're going to listen to it and nurture it and love it and tell it that it is good and that it is smart and that it is right. And soon it will grow. It will grow and grow inside of you until it is big enough to overtake you. It will grow out of control. You will not be able to go a SINGLE DAY without feeling like the walls have closed in and you will never break free. The little voice you nurtured has become a deafening roar!

And this is where the journey begins.

You will begin to feel this immense sense of desperation. You won't simply want the things you want. You will feel that if you don't get these things, your life will be meaningless, and all the pain and torment will be for nothing. And then suddenly all of your choices will have been stripped away. You won't see 175 salad dressings in front of you.

You'll see only two choices: get what you want OR don't get what you want.

From there, for the first time, your path will become clear and all the small decisions you make will be in aid of this one big decision. At least it can be, if you want it to be. This very special feeling called desperation at this very special place called rock bottom could be the best thing that ever happened to you.

It was for me.

Rock bottom for me happened during the summer of 2014. Don't get me wrong. I am maybe the luckiest person in the world in a lot of ways. I was born in the twentieth century to well-off parents and I was fortunate to get a job doing something very cool. At the time I hit rock bottom I was out of the country. I was staying at a beautiful hotel. Things should have been great, but this is where my life finally reached its lowest low. But before I get to that night, I want to tell you how I got there...

The advice I just gave you, about creating your own personal demons and letting them torment you until you feel like you live in hell? That didn't come out of nowhere. I did that to myself. I didn't know I was doing it at the time, but in retrospect, it was an unbelievably important part of my personal development. And, no, it wasn't part of a plan. It was a great big clusterfuck that I somehow managed to turn into a change in my life that led me to where I am today, writing a book that you have somehow gotten this far into. (Unless you skipped pages, in which case GO BACK and read the rest, maybe buy another copy and give it to a friend, I put a lot of energy into this.)

It really started when I was about fourteen. My family took a trip to Mexico. I don't really remember much about it, except for these two words: "strawberry daiquiri." I was always a relatively "good kid," so my family didn't worry about me when I wandered off. But at our little all-inclusive resort in Mexico, no one, including the staff, seemed to care about age limits. I don't even know why I ordered a drink. I'm not sure how I got that idea. No one in my family really drank, other than maybe an occasional glass or two of wine at dinner. But, man, did I like that sugary, icy garbage. More than that, though, I loved the feeling I got after I had two of them. Things seemed to matter a little less. I became a little less scared. I cared less about the fact that I was chubby and insecure and wore a T-shirt in the pool. Imagine that: only fourteen years old and already falling victim to being afraid of my own insecurities and using alcohol (or whatever else) to mask them instead of dealing with them or learning from them.

I was a wacky-ass little kid. Probably super annoying. And me after a few daiquiris was probably no different to my family than me before a few daiquiris. Over the years, I lost my taste for super sweet, gross, faux-tropical drinks, but my taste for feeling better about myself was only beginning to grow.

Cut to my midtwenties. Drinking was no longer something I was doing for fun or to escape from a particular situation. It was my medicine and I used it for everything. I started drinking very heavily every day. I started going out (I had just enough money to afford cabs and luckily was too scared to drive drunk). By the time my late twenties came around, an average night consisted of at least one bottle of wine before dinner, a bottle of wine with dinner, and then a cab somewhere to get whiskey and try to meet women (almost always unsuccessfully because I was insecure and ugly on the outside and on the inside and out of shape and sad and uncomfortable and drunk). Then I would come home alone at two a.m. and drink another few glasses of wine before falling asleep on my couch. Unfortunately, this wasn't every once in a while; this was usually four to five nights a week. The two or three other nights weren't that radically different, but at least I would usually make it into my bed.

By the time I was thirty, I was averaging four bottles of wine, or a bottle of tequila, or a bottle of vodka per day. Every day. I was sick. I never felt well. I would pass out at parties. Some mornings I would wake up with hazy memories of the night before.

In May of that year I went to a friend's thirtieth birthday party. I was alone and sad and scared and knew that I was out of control. I was killing myself and because I was so prideful, instead of trying to stop it, I tried to feel like there was honor in being a party to my own demise. At the celebration, a friend of my friend pulled me aside and told me what he thought I was doing to myself. He was an ER doctor and he said he had a good deal of experience with "people like me." Of course I was aghast that someone would try to tell me anything about myself, even though I definitely knew he was right to call me out. He told me that my eyes looked a little yellow, and he asked me about my drinking habits. I was honest with him. He shrugged and in the least dramatic tone possible said that I was probably going to die soon. I laughed. But he'd seen that reaction before. Nothing about me was new to him.

That was more of a wake-up call than anything. It's one thing when people you love tell you they care about you and make you feel special and important. It just makes you feel good. Their unconditional love is the best fucking enabler there is. But this guy didn't give a shit about me. He didn't make me feel loved and special. He made me feel exactly as I should have felt in that moment: boring, ordinary, and predictable. A walking statistic. Fuck, it burned.

Of course, I wasn't fully ready to admit much of anything. "I can moderate a bit, I guess," I said. He told me just to watch out if any part of my body started to turn yellow. Once that happened I didn't have much longer left, probably. That sounded crazy to me. What did he know? People don't turn yellow.

Until they do.

So that brings us back to the summer of 2014. Our story begins in the very early morning hours. It was about three a.m. when I finally finished off my second bottle of tequila and stumbled back into my hotel room. I immediately fell asleep. But two hours later I woke up with a swirling head and a full bladder. But I wasn't a little bit drunk. I was fucked up. So, with my pants around my ankles, I wandered around the room trying to find my way to the bathroom. But I couldn't find it. I just couldn't. So I gave up. I gathered up the clothes I had worn the previous day. A pair of shorts, some socks, and a T-shirt, and I piled them into an empty corner of the room. Then, without even a second thought, I peed into my new homemade toilet. And then I went back to sleep.

When I woke up a few hours later, my room smelled of piss and sadness. It didn't take long for me to remember what I'd done. I'd been fucked up many, many times before, but this felt different than all the other times. It just felt really pathetic. I felt bad for myself. I felt embarrassed for myself. I hated the idea that I'd done something I didn't want anyone to know about. Who you are in private is who you are. And I was a fucking drunk. I was a pathetic, sick, and devout alcoholic who peed all over his own fucking clothes because he couldn't find a toilet. I was supposed to be a professional. I was supposed to be a leader. I was supposed to be an adult and a boyfriend and a partner and a lover. I was none of those things. I was the embodiment of everything I despised. I was weak. I was a loser.

And then things got worse.

I got into the shower and started to wipe down my aching body. That's when I saw it. The right side of my body looked like someone had drawn all over it with a bright yellow highlighter. Did it happen overnight? Had it been there for days? For weeks? Who knows? I was the only person who would have seen it and I wasn't a trustworthy source. But I knew it was time to make a choice.

This was my rock bottom. This was desperation. I had to make a decision. All the other decisions in my life didn't matter anymore. Where I wanted to live and what I wanted to do when I grew up and what I wanted to eat for dinner didn't matter anymore. My only choice was between life and death.

It wasn't an easy choice to make.

Death represented all the things I knew. Death was going to be easy. I could just keep doing everything I'd been doing. No one knew I was so sad, so pitiful, so diseased. I could keep hiding it. All I had to do was nothing. I could have fun; I could keep drinking and masking my insecurities and only existing for a third of every day. That would be easy. And then I would die and I wouldn't have to worry about any of this shit anymore. People would feel bad for me. They would think about how pained I must have been. My funeral would've been well attended and I would've been fondly remembered by those who knew me and people would've said things like, "This really puts things in perspective" and "Everything happens for a reason."

Living represented everything I was afraid of. Quitting drinking didn't just mean not putting alcohol in my mouth anymore. It meant having to live with myself. It meant feeling my feelings. It meant being responsible for all of my actions, and never having excuses the next day. It meant being uncomfortable, and having no place to hide. And life would go on forever and ever, and I would be sad and afraid and insecure for all of it. Life didn't seem like a good idea.

I can't lie. I don't know why I made the decision I made. But I stood in that shower and I cried and then I got out of the shower and I haven't had a drink since then.

That day changed everything for me. All my decisions were now about one thing. They were made in support of the core decision that I'd reached when I was at my rock bottom. When I was at the peak of my desperation, I decided what I wanted my life to be, and since then, everything has been in aid of that. And everything has been better. I have a lot of the things I want. And the things I don't have yet I will have later.

Now, I'm not saying that quitting drinking is what made me happy. That's just my example. I actually think drinking is great. I think it's tasty and fun and if you can control yourself, then there's nothing better than a couple of glasses of wine over dinner or a few beers on your porch. But my decision wasn't about alcohol. My decision was about living.

I chose to have the life I wanted, no matter how hard or how painful. And you should too.

I hope you don't have the same experience as me. It was terrible. Believe me, there is much worse out there, but this was no fun either. But don't fear rock bottom. Rock bottom shouldn't be a place you wind up at; it should be the place you buy a plane ticket to. Rock bottom is a somewhere you should fully inhabit. Don't let it happen to you. Make it happen for you.

My desperation was the thing that turned my life around. Find yours. Find your rock bottom. You don't have to create it with your life, but you can choose to feel it with your mind. When you get there, you'll know. And then you need to decide to have the life you want. And then you will.

You can't stop yourself from feeling your feelings. And you shouldn't try. Feel them, use them, and become the person you want to be. Use all of the beautiful tools that **FAILURE** gives you:

Shame

Anxiety

Desperation

S.A.D.

These things can't control you anymore. These aren't hurdles. These are the building blocks you need to create a less shitty life than the one you have.

Now that you can see a path forward, I hope you feel a little better.

that was a test. i don't hope you feel
better. don't fall for it!

anxiety!

With over thirty years in the spotlight and twelve years of starring in one of television's top shows, you might assume Jon Cryer has gotten used to being in the spotlight. In some ways he has, but he's still the same guy he was growing up. "I'm still frightened. Every time I have to give a performance or do an appearance I am shook to the core of my being."

From a very early age, Jon was driven by his anxiety. "The negative emotion that spurred me to do things was anxiety. My love of the theater and love of performance is all just an instrument to overcome my crippling anxiety." But he didn't let it control him. He used it. "Anxiety created my style of performing. I play characters that are frightened of things." After *Two and a Half Men* ended, Jon was faced with a flood of opportunities and choices. In trying to approach everything with a yes, he had "forgotten how much anxiety has been a part of [my] psychological makeup...part of me is afraid if I lost it, I wouldn't be as good a performer."

Anxiety often doesn't limit itself to career troubles. "I have terrible anxiety about being a parent and I love my kids. I'm always worried about what I'm doing wrong." If how Jon dealt with his other anxieties is any indication, this particular anxiety is exactly what makes him an excellent and successful parent.

Jon is grateful for his anxiety, but he doesn't believe it to be part of some great plan. "Thinking everything happens for a reason is a very comforting way to look at things. It's chaos. As humans we impose narratives on things so we can feel better about them. It's not real. It's how we choose to interpret it. It's comforting, so we impose narrative cohesion on our lives. Sometimes life just isn't like that."

chapter ten

other people are even worse than you

If you've made it this far, you're doing great (but still not that great). It means you're willing to change. It means you're willing to accept that you're not as great as the world has told you that you are. But you've also taken a beating. It's supposed to be hard. No one ever told you that excelling would be easy. And as we've already seen, there are very few bullshit phrases that really hold up to scrutiny, but one I will carry to the grave with me is "If it's easy, it isn't worth doing."

You should be demoralized. If you've been honest with yourself, you probably feel like you're kind of a piece of shit. How can a piece of shit like you really make it in this world? Shouldn't you give up?

No, you fucking idiot. You shouldn't.

And why not?

Because almost everyone out there is an even bigger piece of shit than you are. All the people you're in competition with have all the same problems you have, but what they don't have is the new knowledge that you have. They don't know they're not great. You do. You now have a leg up on them in a huge way.

Take an honest look around. People are pretty terrible. Read your Facebook feed for a few minutes (if you can do that without setting yourself on fire). I would guess that less than 10 percent of people you know ever have any idea what's going on in the world around them. And those people probably only have it together 10 percent of the time. Using those statistics, it's fair to estimate that only 1 percent of the people you're talking to are even remotely making any sense ever. That means there's a 99 percent chance you've got your shit together more than the person you're communicating with. I mean, don't get me wrong, you're still a piece of garbage, BUT you're less of a piece of garbage than them.

Simply by realizing your lack of worth, you have a head start when it comes to identifying challenges and overcoming them. No one is thinking about how to fix themselves; they're making all the same mistakes that you used to make. It's a miraculous time to be a self-critical human being in this world. You can learn and grow every minute and dig your roots deeper and deeper into the enriching soil as your competitors bask in the sun and think about how green their leaves are. By not needing to FEEL great, you may BECOME great. (Probably not but, you know, maybe.)

Life is a competition, and there isn't enough of anything to go around. In order to get your share you need to stop thinking that other people are better or more gifted or more magical unicorns. You've stopped thinking this way about yourself and now you must stop thinking this way about others.

Now is where you get to take a break from being self-critical and you get to have a little bit of fun.

You've earned this. Don't feel bad. Don't hold back. Go for it!

○ What are the worst qualities about your mother?
What are the worst qualities about your father?
What are the worst qualities about your siblings?
○ What are the worst qualities about your significant
other?

Okay, those are people you love so it may be a little hard to really DIG THE FUCK IN AND DESTROY THEM. FINE. Let's make it a little easier.

○ What are the worst qualities about your boss?
What are the worst qualities about your least favorite acquaintance?
What are the worst qualities about your least favorite coworker?
○ What are the worst qualities about your favorite ex?
What are the worst qualities about your least favorite ex?
○ What are the worst qualities about your least favorite person on Earth?

A little bit easier, right? These are the people who inhabit your world. Don't you feel like you have a leg up on them? Even if you suck, don't they suck more?

I said that this was supposed to be fun. I can tell you from personal experience that the only thing that comes even close to feeling as good as getting what you want is watching someone who's been a jerk to you lose. Gore Vidal said it best: "It is not enough to succeed. Others must fail."

In some ways this may seem mean-spirited, and, yes, in many ways it is, but sometimes a little meanness pointed in the right direction is okay. After all, everything in life is a competition, and not just the obvious things.

The job you want. The life partner you want. The painting you want. If they're great, which they should be, there are going to be a lot of people who want them. If you marry someone wonderful, you are effectively making someone wonderful unavailable to everyone else, and if someone else marries someone wonderful, they are making that person unavailable to you. What if there is a limited amount of "good" in the world? What if not everyone can have what *they* want? What if good people, good art, good jobs, exist in finite numbers like commodities? We'll be out of oil soon. What if we run out of all the other good things too?

It's not the most romantic way to look at life, but I'm pretty sure it's true. All the things you want are limited. Competition is good. The evil voice that lives inside you isn't always going to be powerful enough to compel you to get to your goals. Once in a while you're going to have to make another human your enemy. You can choose to compete in any way you want. You can play dirty or you can play clean. Truthfully, there are many ways to fight for what you want (I advise you to play honest and not hurt anyone along the way, lest you end up in someone else's crosshairs a few years down the road), but the important thing to remember is that your enemies have all the weaknesses that you've just shed.

They are incorrectly confident. They are regretless. They are acting as if they know what they are doing. Learn to read the weaknesses and just remember not to be like them. Never stand down because you think someone is better than you. Chances are they're just playing the part so people like you don't encroach on their territory.

You are a new kind of person now. You are no longer held down by the earthly fears and insecurities that plague everyone around you. You have an arsenal of weapons and you should feel very good about that. Use these skills whenever you can. Carpet-bomb the competition.

But never forget who you love. Treat them differently. Teach them your new skills. Use your skills to help them get what they want too.

REMINDER: you love maybe like ten people on Earth. There are about seven billion people you don't love. So, at the very least, you feel better than most of those seven billion people. Enjoy it, but only enjoy it for a second. Quickly discard this information lest you start feeling really good about yourself and turning yourself back into the monster you used to be. This information is only to be used in case of emergencies. Tuck it deep, but don't forget it. You're bad, but you can still win, because other people are worse.

Before we leave this chapter, I think it's important for you to remember what Uncle Ben told Peter Parker: "With great power comes great responsibility." You are a machine now. You have the ability to achieve your own desires and wishes so much more efficiently at this point. This also gives you a greater ability to love and to altruistically throw success at those who are less fortunate than you and those who are not in direct competition with you.

I feel bad (not really) telling you this, but now that you are capable of changing your world at will, you are also capable of changing the world for other people. You have inherited great (and in my opinion, obvious) skills, and you are now beholden to use those skills to improve the world around you. But don't think I'm asking you to be some kind of altruistic superhuman. You live in the world and the people you love live in the world. Make the world better as an act of selfishness. Make it better for you and the ones you love. If other people's lives improve as a by-product of that, well, you're just going to have to live with that.

It is only by introducing yourself to the parts of the world that need your help that you can further expand your knowledge. Improve yourself by listening. This is another thing people just don't take the time to do. Open your ears and shut your mouth and you will suddenly feel something new, a little bit of light entering your cold, black heart. Admitting you don't know what others experience lets you learn from the experiences of others. This is part of your continuing education as a human being. Just because you're not great doesn't mean you have to be dumb and shitty.

And while others may not be great, they still have a whole hell of a lot to teach you.

rejection!

You'd be hard-pressed to find an actor with a more diverse résumé than Paul Scheer. He's starred in movies, created beloved television series, and was part of the longest-running off-Broadway comedy in history. These are all crowded arenas. So how does Paul Scheer find a way to always thrive?

"In a creative position, you are driven by competition: the desire to do as well as your peers and continuously impress them so that you stay relevant and on their level. It's a constant game of subconscious one-upmanship that actually makes the entire community better for it. Now obviously it's not all competition. You are creating because you love what you do, but if art isn't constantly evolving, or inspiring you to do better, then why do it at all? We all want to keep building on the shoulders of the people before us no matter what area we are in."

Much of the creative process has a basis in love, but tapping into that can be more complicated. "The times of the highest anxiety, the highest stress, the times I've been the most depressed, I've made the best art out of those moments. When I had a devastating breakup, I had a year of creativity that was unbelievable. I was blossoming. You're putting that anger, all that FUCK THIS, MY LIFE SUCKS, I'm pissed off, and if you can harness that rage you can actually create something good."

Before Paul Scheer became a go-to name for all things comedy, he had some harder times. "When I auditioned for *SNL* and didn't get it, I felt terrible. Whenever you don't get something big, you think, 'That was my shot, I missed it.' What a rejection of me on the one thing I am. I am NOT GOOD ENOUGH. Those are very powerful motivators. If you feel like you as a human being isn't good enough, then it's like the training montage in *Rocky*.

"Rocky is fueled by negative emotion. He gets his ass kicked and says fuck I need to chase chickens. Rocky has been told by everybody, 'You're a piece of shit, you're nothing, you'll never compete. You're not good enough.' So it makes you prove that you're good enough. If you access the negative emotions in the right way, you challenge yourself to get even better."

And some things don't change in people. "Look at Rocky now. He's still fighting people. 'Fuck you, man, you can't fight anymore...' These are the people that succeed. Being underestimated is the best chance to get ahead."

And it's not just Rocky. You don't always have to be the hero. "Luke Skywalker is alone. Darth Vader is surrounded by people he loves, cool cars, he's a pretty good dude." Anyone who has met Paul knows he's one of the good guys, not one of the bad guys. But like many others, he has found a way to access and harness his negative emotions to become better.

"Stress and anxiety breed creativity."

chapter eleven

you'll be dead soon

I'm going to keep this short and sweet. Every day you're alive is unearned. Every day you exist on Earth is a fucking miracle. Your parents made you and raised you (or didn't) without your permission. But now you're here. You'll be dead soon. But you're not dead yet.

That truly won't last forever. Every time you drive down the freeway you're trusting that all those other people out there won't just cross the median and kill you. Every time you eat at a restaurant you're trusting that the chef won't accidentally poison you. Every time you close your eyes you're trusting that a psychotic stranger won't stab you in the fucking face and make a mask out of your skin.

This life is temporary. Death is permanent. You will do very few things while you are here on Earth but you will do NOTHING forever. Don't waste your time here doing nothing. There is plenty of time for that while you chill in the ground until the cemetery you ended up in gets turned into a Walmart.

Life is glorious. Life is full of adventure. Life is full of limitless opportunity.

Don't waste it. Don't wait. There is no promise of tomorrow.

Figure out what the fuck you want to do and fucking do it. Get out there and make your life happen. No one else is going to do it for you. No one else cares about your self-actualization. I don't care about your success. I wrote this book for me. I wrote it because it was what I needed to do with my thoughts. If you use it to make your life better, let me know, and I'll feel better for thirty seconds about my life, but then we will both move on.

As I write these last few words, I feel a great deal of accomplishment, but by the time you read these words, I won't feel that anymore. That feeling doesn't help me. It doesn't help me get better and it doesn't help me grow and it doesn't make my life happen for me.

So, don't do this for me, don't do it for your mother or your father or your sister or your annoying aunt who won't stop asking you when you're going to get your shit together. Do it for you.

Do it because there is no other choice. Do it because you'll win or you'll die. You WILL be dead soon so just fucking get started on living.

And as you take your new knowledge and begin to navigate the mysterious waters of life, take your sadness, take your rage, take your fear, take your failure, take your desperation, take your pain, take your anxiety (take your medication), and make all of those things work *for* you, not *against* you.

And no matter what happens, you must always remember this one thing:

You're Not That Great.

epilogue

Over the last year, I've talked to or interviewed many people about the topics in this book. While I feel like everyone I look up to, and I truly mean *everyone*, has some experience in using negative emotions to their benefit, there are two people who've said things to me about their transitions out of this method of thinking that I found more important than their thoughts on the topic of negativity itself. These two people couldn't be more different, but they've both been outspoken about their troubled times. And they are both people who have persevered and fought through to become the kind of artists I admire. I want to share their thoughts with you. If this book is all about where we are, where we've been, and where we are going, these quotes are about where we may eventually find ourselves, if everything works out.

I just had a bite of this amazing Turkish cotton candy I found at a place I shop...It's sweet and has flecks of pistachio and is dense yet light and just amazing. And I thought, Would I like this if there was also stuff in it that tasted terrible, that made me sick, that just tasted like filth? No. It would no longer be good. Negative emotions are the filth in the thing that tastes good, to me. Maybe they have their place, maybe they have to be dealt with, but for the most part I keep them as far away from the daily fare as possible.

—John Darnielle (singer-songwriter, The Mountain Goats)

In my mind, fear is disabling. For me, insecurity and an elevated focus on and concern for an economic insecurity I grew up with propelled me in many ways. I try to remember that feelings are not facts. And although, by and large, I am entitled to my feelings, I try not to allow them to guide me like I once did. Those underdog feelings can motivate you. But one day you turn around and see that you aren't the underdog anymore. So it's time to take that label off.

—Alec Baldwin (actor)

acknowledgments

First and foremost, thank you to every single asshole out there who ever said or did anything mean to me. You are forever in my thoughts. Fuck you to hell and back.

To my agent, Jess Regel at Foundry: you helped take an idea that lived in my mind and you turned it into a thing that can be held. That is miraculous. You are a wizard.

To my editor, Maddie Caldwell at Grand Central: you took a wild clusterfuck of words and molded them into something more meaningful to me than I could have ever imagined. You are impressive in every way.

To my amazing team, Christina Kuo and David Fox and Jessica Bergman: I would be so damn lost without your help and your guidance. Thank you for being my spirit guides.

To my friends: Aron and Matthew and Peter and Heather and Bill and James and Jennifer and Pete and Cassie and Nicole and Bennett and Amanda and Tommy. You are the people who keep me sane but also let me be crazy. You are so important to me and I love you so much.

To my *Bachelor* family: every single one of you has made the last decade of my life so tremendously interesting. We have traveled the world together, and along the way it has been the relationships we've had that have given me the greatest joy. Thank you for letting me be a little part of your lives.

To the people who have encouraged me along the way: Matt and John and Bobby and Iliza and Jenny and Jomny and Brannon and Jordan and Derek and Jason and Ben and Nick and Rachel and JoJo and Craig and Abigail and Bethany and Meghan and Ali and Chris and Andi and Jared and Fitz and Mike and Flula and Travon and Kelly and Chad and Michael and Tim and Bobby and Paul and Jon and Erin and Molly and Meegan and Mark and Scott and Sean and Catherine and JP and Ashley and Ashleigh and AshLeaux and Kaitlyn and Shawn and Courtney and Paul and Rob and Jen and Jenn and Jade and Tanner and Carly and Evan and Mike and Martin and Leigh and Corbett and Mike and Kate and another Chris and Barret and Marc and Pam and Isaac and Rachel and Bobak and Yassir and of course Nick Cave and the Bad Seeds.

To Molly: every day with you is better than the last. I am devastatingly in love with you.

To my sisters, Tal and Shir: thank you for making me aim so high. You two were so cool and kicked so much ass it inspired me to just try to keep up.

To my father, Robert: thank you for being strange and difficult and brilliant. I think some of it rubbed off.

Most of all, to my mother, Tamar: I do pretty much everything I do because I want to make you proud. You're the strongest person I've ever met. Thank you for never letting me give up.